HOTEL MANAGEMENT

Encyclopaedia of Hotel, Tourism and Hospitality Management in 21st Century Series

HOTEL MANAGEMENT

Edited by

Amrik Singh Sudan

ANMOL PUBLICATIONS PVT. LTD.

NEW DELHI - 110 002 (INDIA)

ANMOL PUBLICATIONS PVT. LTD.
Regd. Office: 4360/4, Ansari Road, Daryaganj,
New Delhi-110 002 (India)
Ph.: 23278000, 23261597
Branch Office: No. 1015, Ist Main Road, BSK IIIrd Stage
IIIrd Phase, IIIrd Block,
Bangalore-560 085 (India)
Tel.: 080-41723429
Visit us at: www.anmolpublications.com

Hotel Management

First Published, 2002
Reprint, 2005
ISBN 81-261-1066-X

PRINTED IN INDIA

Published by J.L. Kumar for Anmol Publications Pvt. Ltd., New Delhi - 110 002 and Printed at Mehra Offset Press, Delhi.

Contents

Preface

Hotel industry has close relation with tourism industry. With the flourishing of international tourism, Hotel industry has also gone drastic changes and has grown leaps and bound. In the current age of globalisation and liberalisation it is growing rapidly—having cosmopolitan touch. In true sense, hotel, hospitality and catering are enthusing the feeling of international integration, thus the world as a global village.

The present work is intended to bring together authentic information on diverse aspects of hotel, hospitality, and catering management such as—hotel management, restaurant management, housekeeping management, hospitality marketing, food and beverage management, and foodservice operations. The entire information is logically organised under above titles. The concepts and developments are supported by facts and figures.

To make the work comprehensive we have gathered the information from various sources. We are grateful to all the scholars whose writings are cited or substantially made use of in the present venture. I am also thankful to my colleagues and friends who have assisted me in one way or other while preparing the manuscript. Last but not the least, I am indebted to Mr. J.L. Kumar, Managing Director, Anmol Publications Pvt. Ltd., New Delhi for his constant moral support and also for bringing out this work within a short span of time.

—Editor

1

Introduction

The word "modern" is loaded with the potential for much misunderstanding. Hotels are changing and will continue to change. As a result, the techniques of management of modem hotels have to adapt to changing circumstances. When modem hotel organizations are addressed in a later section, we will confront some of the issues that dictate and influence this change in a modem hotel organization.

Like many other American businesses, hotels have been affected by shifts in emphasis among the country's *living patterns.* People and industry have moved from the so-called rust belt to the sun belt. There has been a concentration of hotel activities in reborn and reconstructed central cities This can be contrasted with the suburban and interstate highway interchange hotel and motel construction boom of the 1950s and 1960s.

Demographics also play a role in this regard and will continue to influence the foreseeable future. As the baby boom generation and its children mature, the population of the country will for many years be older, healthier, and better educated than previous generations.

Technology in the form of computers and labour-saving mechanical equipment has had and will continue to have a major effect on the way in which hotels are managed and operated.

The concept of *market segmentation*, increasingly finely tuned market definitions, will dictate hotel structures, organizations, and management tactics that are designed to pay particular attention to those market segments.

The well-documented change in the complexion of the *national economy* from an emphasis on goods to one on services has kindled a number of new ideas about the way in which we manage the design and delivery of these services. Hotels, restaurants, and travel services are now seen as unique entities that dictate special kinds of managerial techniques and strategies.

Changes in people's *travel patterns* have also altered the way in which we manage our hotel properties. Deregulation of the airlines has driven a change in the way millions of people travel each year with the hub and spoke design of airline services.

Many hotel companies are now locating major hotel properties adjacent to hub air transport facilities, taking advantage of the fact that business travellers may not need to travel to a central business district (CBD) to accomplish their purposes in a given area. Meetings and conferences can now be scheduled within a five-minute limousine ride from the air terminal, and the business traveller can be back on the plane for his or her next destination before the day is over without having to stay overnight in a CBD hotel.

New *patterns of investment* in hotel facilities have emerged in the last two decades, and more attention is now paid to achieving optimum *return on investment*. Because people from outside the hotel industry are now participating in the financial structuring of the hotel industry, hotel operations are no longer dependent on the vision of a single entrepreneur.

Managers now have to design tactics and strategies to achieve heretofore unanticipated financial goals. This has also altered the complexion of the management and organization of the modern hotel. Most of the foregoing issues and influences still operate, to a greater or lesser extent, on the organizational structures and strategies of the modern hotel.

The difficulties facing hotels in the early 1990s can be directly attributed to the oversupply of hotel rooms fuelled by a boom in hotel construction in the late 1980s. According to Culligan, five main factors supported the construction boom:

1. The passage of the 1981 tax law that allowed generous depreciation, low-interest loans, and other tax shelters;
2. The development of marginally profitable hotel properties by parent chains intent on gaining market presence;
3. The influx of momentary oversupply of funds, particularly foreign, to invest in new or acquired hotels;
4. The creation of a funding vehicle (syndication) that distributed risk to limited partners and generated immediate profits for developers and operators; and
5. The attractiveness of real estate in an inflationary environment and the strength of hotels' financial performance.

Culligan goes on to note that demand in the hotel industry tracks remarkably consistently with the growth in supply and, particularly since 1985, has grown at a relatively unprecedented annual rate of 4.3 percent. The rising demand is not, as Culligan states, easy to explain and is based upon a number of "interrelated variables."

Culligan's inventory of these variables is listed below:

— Employment growth

— Growth in corporate profits

— Expansion of the Gross National Product

— Increased travel by baby boomers (the over-50 segment)

— Increased product-dependent growth emanating from new hotels catering to meetings, conventions, and conferences

— More favourable consumer spending patterns, based on a sustained economic expansion

— Continued softness in fuel prices

— Growth in air travel

— More aggressive and successful merchandising programs designed to capture latent demand (e.g., weekend packages)

— A weakened dollar (discouraging U.S. travel abroad and increasing foreign visitations)

— High employment growth in demand-related segments (nonfinancial service jobs increased 5.3 percent in 1988)

— Increased discretionary income

At this writing, since 1990, it is clear that the interrelated variables that affect hotel demand have changed significantly from the time Culligan wrote his article. In early 1993, for instance, employment growth was stagnant; corporate profits were low; the expansion of the Gross National Product was only a marginal percentage above previous years; and travel among most segments was down due to corporate restructuring, downsizing, or reorganizing. Vast layoffs in the hundreds of thousands have been announced every month. While fuel prices have continued to be relatively stable, consumer spending patterns and high employment growth have not materialized, particularly in light of corporate layoffs and an ongoing nervousness among consumers over whether their financial wherewithal is safe.

Fifty years ago, economist Joseph Schumpter coined the phrase "creative destruction" to describe an underlying dynamic of capitalism, a process in which rapid economic expansion automatically engenders forces that bring about a period of contraction. Doubters of this famous economic axiom need look no further than the hospitality industry for verification.

The creative destruction unleashed in the economy has not limited its effects to the hotel and airline industries. The go-go years of the 1980s have given way to the oh-no 1990s, an era of layoffs, salary freezes, and cutbacks across the spectrum of U.S. businesses—from automotive to computer and publishing industries. But the impact on the airline and hotel sectors has been particularly severe.

Some hotel companies are embracing new corporatewide management strategies to cope with the economic realities of the 1990s. For instance, both the Ritz-Carlton Hotel Company, Atlanta, and the North American division of the Westin Hotel Company are implementing total quality management. Total quality management (TQM) emphasizes quality in all aspects of a company's operations, as well as participatory decision making involving all those affected by the decision—from top management to the lowest-ranking employees. Customer satisfaction defines success, so vendors and customers also are involved in some issues.

Hotel organization structures are not immune to the influences of the economy and business cycles, so the difficulties that befell business in general have also affected hotel organizations, with downsizing or reengineering also hitting hotel companies. In the early 1990s, some hotels eliminated entire levels of management or combined managerial responsibilities so that the organization became flatter. In the typical functional chart the executive assistant manager may be eliminated, making division heads directly responsible to the general manager (GM). Some hotels have eliminated separate managers at the division level, with all department managers reporting directly to the GM.

However this restructuring has occurred, organizations are still formed around principles such as those outlined by Stoner and Wankel. They said that the organizing process involves balancing a company's need for both stability and change. They go on to outline organizing as a multistep process, based on that proposed by Dale.

— Details all the work that must be done to attain the organization's goals.

— Provides for dividing the total work performed into a group of activities that can be performed by one person or a group of people.

— Combines the work of an organization's members in some logical and efficient manner.

— Sets up a mechanism to coordinate the work of the organization members into a unified, harmonious whole.

— Sets up a mechanism to monitor the effectiveness of how well the organization is achieving its goals.

In the modern hotel organization, even a reengineered

one, a linear line and staff structure has emerged to reflect this theoretical organizing process.

Line functions

Hotel employees in line functions have regular or semiregular contact with the organization's guests. The line operations in a hotel organization are the rooms division and food and beverage division.

Obviously, some departmental functions within each line division involve more or less guest contact than others, depending on the nature of the jobs. The underlying commonalty in these cases is that most of these employees are hands-on participants in the assembly and delivery of the hotel's services.

For instance, under most circumstances security people will not have much regular guest contact; housekeeping staff may have somewhat more guest contact; in the rooms division, obviously the front office staff will have the vast majority of guest face-to-fact contact.

In the food and beverage division, as a line division, the employees of the restaurant, bars, room service, and banquet departments will have a tremendous amount of face-to-face guest interaction; however, only under special circumstances and on an irregular basis will the food production staff under the hotel chef interact with the guests.

Staff functions

Staff functions are generally those behind the scenes sorts of activities that support the line functions and, under most circumstances, employees filling these functions have little or no guest contact, although a major component of their job is to influence the quality of a guest's stay. Engineering has been included as a staff function for those reasons

The success of the engineering function heavily influences the quality of the guest's stay. At the same time the other functions of the engineering department support the activities of almost every other department in the hotel. For example, the engineering department maintains and repairs equipment that is crucial to all of the hotel's line functions from the food production equipment in the kitchen, to the tables and chairs in the dining room, the accounting machines, the furniture in the lobby, and the carts that the bellhops use to transport guest luggage.

Viewed in this way, the engineering department can be considered a true staff department that serves and supports at any given time any or all of the other departments in the hotel.

Other typical hotel organization charts will place the engineering department in the rooms division because engineering works best there in the hotel's organization or because of tradition. This situation may also be true for other departments that in the past have been traditionally thought of as rooms division functions. Security is one example.

In some organizations housekeeping has been changed to a staff function rather than one that belongs strictly in the rooms division, for housekeeping by definition keeps the entire house.

Organizations, however, are more than just boxes and charts. The most modem business organization structures have not changed much in form since the Roman Catholic Church first designed the pyramidal structure as a visual depiction of organizational relationships with which we are so familiar today. What does affect organizations, not so much in their pictorial view, but in the way in which the organization responds to external and internal stimuli, can be seen by analysing several of the readings included here and those that are suggested at the end for further study.

Professor Eddystone C. Nebel, III, is the C.B. Smith Professor of Hotel Management at Purdue University. He recently spent a sabbatical leave researching and observing ten outstanding General Managers (GMs) and a total of 53 key subordinates. During his research Professor Nebel gained some critical insights into how hotel organizations function. In his book, *Managing Hotels Effectively: Lessons From Outstanding General Managers* (1991), Nebel weaves together the insights gained from the GMs with organizational theory. He then couples this with the increasingly important role that committees can play in the successful organization. Another view of the particular dynamics of hotel organizations is the Dann and Hornsey analysis of the processes of conflict within a hotel organizational structure. Their discussion highlights the areas in which interdepartmental conflict can and does occur and offers a cogent and provocative explanation of the dynamics of such conflict.

The Glover article treats one of the pathologies of organizational life with a discussion of an inventory of organizational ineffectiveness characteristics. While there is no dearth of literature on hotel organizations, these three sections highlight some of the current thought and research about the relationships between organizational structure, department organizational problems, and the organization's people. Additional insights can be gained from the suggested readings.

Organizational design

This section will review some of the general management principles of organizational design, including the important but often neglected topic of a hotel's meeting structure.

The elements of organizational structure

If the efforts of people in organizations are to be channelled toward productive ends, structure must be given to their activities. Aldag and Stearns list five ways by which managers give structure to organizations:

(1) work specialization,

(2) departmentalization,

(3) patterns of authority,

(4) spans of control, and

(5) methods of coordination.

Whenever a manager decides to make an organizational change, he or she will usually have to take these five elements into account.

Specialization

If there is more than one way to accomplish something, management must make a conscious decision about how to divide tasks among workers. At one extreme is the case of little or no specialization where an individual worker is responsible for all the tasks required to complete a job. An example is the chef in a small country restaurant who single-handedly prepares an entire meal for 20 guests. It's rewarding to have total control over a project and motivating to see the results of one's efforts. The problem, however, is that as the demand for products or services increases, it becomes more difficult for individuals or small groups to increase their output without changing the way they are organized.

One of management's tasks is to determine the extent to which work and jobs should be specialized. As a general rule, specialization holds out the possibility of greater worker productivity and managerial control over tasks.

On the other hand, dividing complete jobs into smaller subunits tends to increase the need for coordinating the activities of numerous workers, each involved in separate, specialized tasks. Also, overspecialization can result in jobs so narrow that workers lose interest, motivation drops, error rates increase, and quality suffers.

Departmentalization

As organizations grow in size, managers are faced with the need to group certain jobs together in order to ensure efficient coordination and control of activities. Most restaurants have chosen to departmentalize with food preparation and food service as separate functional departments. This is a very logical and practical solution. There are distinctly different kinds of work performed in preparing and serving food, both in the process and the function of the two activities. Forming departments along *functional lines* is the most common method of organizing a business.

Authority

Every time managers restructure a job or move members of a group working together into different departments, they are faced with the question of how much decision-making authority to grant individual workers, managers, or departments.

Organizations are never totally centralized or decentralized with regard to decision making. Rather, they tend toward one direction or the other. A number of factors must be taken into account when deciding the pattern of authority that is best for an organization. Managers must consider the experience and personality of subordinates, the environment in which they work, the business strategy to be followed, and the management style with which they feel most comfortable.

Line executives are those who have responsibility over business units that provide products or services to customers and account for the revenues of the business. The rooms and food and beverage departments account for most of a hotel's revenue.

On the other hand, staff departments are set up because the principles of work specialization and departmentalization suggest efficiencies from such an organizational design. The personnel and engineering departments of a hotel are examples of staff units. Once set up, however, staff departments sometimes cause organizational problems.

The basic issue is, how much authority should functional staff executives have over line executives? At one extreme, line executives could be given total authority. At the other extreme, staff executives, in their speciality areas, could be granted authority over line executives. Two examples of positions between these extremes would be:

(1) line executives would be required to consult with staff specialists only before making a decision, and

(2) line and staff executives would be required to make joint decisions.

Whatever the situation, top executives such as hotel general managers (GMs) must arbitrate line-staff disputes when they develop.

Spans of control

Spans of control relate to the number of subordinates reporting to a supervisor. In the past, some management scholars advocated an ideal span of control of exactly seven subordinates. That simplistic view is no longer held. The ideal span of control is dependent on:

— Task similarity-the more similar the tasks of subordinates, the wider the span of control can be.

— Training and professionalism-the more trained and skilled a subordinate, the less supervision required and the greater the span of control can be.

— Task certainty-the more routine and predictable the work tasks, the greater the span of control can be.

— Frequency of interaction-if relationships require frequent interaction, the span of control must be narrow.

— Task integration-the more a supervisor must integrate and coordinate the tasks of subordinates, the narrower the span of control must be.

— Physical dispersion-the more widely dispersed subordinates are, the fewer a manager can properly supervise.

Some of these factors may work in opposite directions. For example, fast food restaurants are operationally quite similar to each other, suggesting a broad span of control. However, their physical dispersion works in the opposite direction of limiting span of control.

Coordination of activities

Problems arise when organizations do not properly coordinate their activities. In simple organizations of only a few people, coordination is usually not a major concern. Problems develop, however, as organizations grow in complexity.

Work specialization and departmentalization are organizational responses to a business's growth. As duties are subdivided, it becomes increasingly important to coordinate the activities of individuals and groups toward common goals. The kind of coordination required depends on how various tasks and activities are linked together. These linkages result in a variety of different kinds of interdependence between individuals and groups.

Pooled interdependence refers to activities that can be performed with little interaction between individuals or groups. Suppose a hotel has three telephone operators. Each can usually perform the required duties independently (that is, without any interaction with the others), as can room maids and cashiers at food outlets.

Because these workers need not interact among themselves, coordination of their activities is best accomplished by proscribing standardized rules and procedures for each to follow, by intensive individual training, and by direct supervision. The role of coordination is to ensure that each independently performed task is carried out at the same level of efficiency and quality.

Sequential interdependence occurs when one task's output becomes a second task's input. This is typical of production-line operations, where products are progressively assembled. A hotel example is the guest checkin process. The "output" of a front desk becomes an "input" to the accounting department in the form of a guest billing record, or folio.

A well-planned system linking the rooms department and the accounting department is needed for this activity to go smoothly. Proper coordination is ensured through detailed planning, scheduling, and standardization.

Coordination also requires identification of the linkages that exist between activities. Still greater coordination is required in cases where the output of Unit A is input for Unit B, and the output of Unit B is input for Unit A. Whenever there is a high level of interaction between work units they are said to exhibit *reciprocal interdependence.*

One example is the coordination needed to host a major convention. Rooming decisions made by the front desk must be coordinated with accounting, sales, housekeeping, and reservations; function room usage requires interaction between convention services, engineering, food and beverage, and accounting. Because any one department's output and activity affect numerous other departments, mutual adjustments among each are required.

Close coordination is only possible through *direct communication* and joint decision making between the units involved. While standardized plans and procedures are helpful, they cannot possibly solve all the problems resulting from such a high degree of departmental interaction. Direct communication and group meetings become a necessity to ensure proper coordination when activities involve reciprocal interdependence.

Static principles of organizational design

Experience has accumulated for centuries about how to organize institutions such as government bureaucracies, the military, religions, large commercial trading companies, and since the industrial revolution, large manufacturing concerns.

A number of principles regarding how to structure organizations have been developed. While these principles do not hold in all circumstances, they are important and should be understood and applied where appropriate.

Chain of command

A hotel's organizational chart depicts the chain of

command. It should be possible for any employee to trace his or her way up the organization chart's chain of command all the way to the GM. The typical pyramid shape of an organization chart is consequence of the chain of command and the span of control concept discussed previously. Chain of command is a very powerful concept. It provides structure in an organization by setting forth a system of subordinate-superior accountability for everyone.

The chain of command affects communication within organizations for both subordinates and superiors. If a GM wants to make a change in housekeeping, chain-of-command considerations would have the GM communicate through the rooms department manager, who in turn will speak to the director of housekeeping.

The traditional chain-of-command structure in a hotel would have the baker responsible to the chef and the chef responsible to the food and beverage director. Accordingly, the baker should communicate with the chef and not directly with the food and beverage director. While it is important to be aware of possible chain-of-command problems, too strict an adherence to this principle can take away the spontaneity in an organization.

Experienced hotel GMs often break with this principle, but in a way that is not harmful to the hotel. The immediacy of some problems in hotels sometimes requires hotel executives to issue orders directly to subordinates two or more levels down in the organization.

GMs may also want to maintain personal control over some project or aspect of the hotel and choose to bypass immediate subordinates in order to do so. This does little harm as long as everyone knows what is happening and the organizational climate is otherwise healthy and trusting.

Unity of command

This principle states that each employee is responsible to one and only one superior. That is, each person has only one boss. Unity of command is violated quite regularly in most organizations.

A hotel waitress, whose boss is the restaurant manager, might be corrected for a safety violation by a safety officer who reports to the personnel director. The waitress feels as if she has two bosses and, in effect, she does.

This common problem occurs as organizations grow in size and task specialization takes place. Specialists in safety (or accounting, personnel, data processing, and so on) often do have authority in their speciality area over workers who do not report directly to them through the chain of command.

Problems can develop because of conflicting orders from more than one boss. The solution is not necessarily to eliminate specialization and staff positions but rather to ensure, by closely coordinating activities, that order rather than confusion reigns. The GM plays a key role in effecting coordination throughout the hotel.

Delegation

Young managers often find delegation a difficult task to master. A subordinate's ability to successfully carry out an assignment depends in part on the clarity of his or her superior's delegation instructions.

Delegation can range from assigning a minor task to a subordinate to granting complete responsibility for a major undertaking. It's important for both superior and subordinate to understand and agree on the level of responsibility, the freedom of action, and the amount of authority that accompanies a delegated task. There are various levels of delegation, each of which is useful in different circumstances. Here are some examples of orders that result in different degrees of delegation:

(1) gather information for my decision,

(2) set out two or three alternatives; I'll then choose,

(3) make a recommendation for my approval,

(4) make a decision but inform me of it before proceeding,

(5) take action but inform me of it before proceeding, and

(6) take action on your own; it's not necessary to communicate with me regarding this matter.

The extent to which authority is delegated depends in part on the experience of the subordinate. Young, inexperienced subordinates can expect only limited delegation until they have proven themselves. The amount of authority delegated will usually increase as trust between superior and subordinate is built. It's been said that when a person becomes a manager he or she gives up earning an honest living.

Hotel managers don't usually make beds, cook food, or provide service directly to guests. Rather, their job is to see to it that the organization they manage provides proper guest services.

Hotel functional organizational design

Individual hotels are usually organized along functional lines with departments grouped according to the particular work activity in which they are engaged. The hotel is divided along functional lines into five separate administrative departments: rooms, food and beverage, sales and marketing, personnel, and accounting. The five department heads report directly to the GM. Each department is further subdivided into smaller organizational units. These subdivisions represent additional refinements of the work performed and the knowledge and skills of the people in each subunit.

The rooms department

The rooms department performs the lodging function of a hotel. Reservations must be accepted, guests must be hospitably received and assigned clean rooms, the status of available and occupied rooms must be kept current, guests must receive mail and phone messages promptly, security must be maintained, public spaces such as lobbies must be kept clean, and guest questions must be answered. These are some of the important functions of the rooms department.

The rooms department is divided into a number of subunits, each of which performs rather specialized tasks. In many instances, these subunits are also referred to as departments. For example, the laundry department, which in a 500-room hotel is quite large, is responsible for cleaning and pressing all the hotel's linens and employee uniforms as well as guest laundry. Its function is extremely specialized.

Little of the knowledge and skills required to manage a laundry operation are transferable to other areas of hotel operations. The front office is where guests are greeted when they arrive at the hotel, where they're registered, and where they're assigned to a room. Telephone operators and other guest communications functions usually fall under the front office department. The hotel's bell staff is also part of this department.

Reservations takes and keeps track of a hotel's

future bookings. The housekeeping department is responsible for cleaning guest rooms and public spaces. Security is responsible for guest safety. Finally, the engineering department is responsible for the operation and maintenance of the hotel's entire physical plant, including electrical, mechanical, heating, air conditioning and ventilation, structure, and plumbing. It also performs minor repairs and renovations.

A great deal of interdependence exists within the rooms department, thus calling for close coordination of activities between subunits. Linkages exist between the front office and the reservations department. Reservations must inform the front office of the number of presold rooms each day to ensure that a current inventory of rentable rooms is always available.

Conversely, the front office must let reservations know whenever walk-in guests (those without reservations) are registered. Linkages also exist between the front office and housekeeping, Information regarding room status must flow both ways:

When a guest checks out, the front office must inform housekeeping so the room may be cleaned. Once a room is cleaned, housekeeping must inform the front office so that it may be sold. These are both examples of reciprocal interdependence in which individual units provide each other with inputs.

Other linkages within the rooms department are illustrative of sequential interdependence, which occurs when the output of one unit becomes the input of another.

An example is housekeeping's inability to properly provision a guest room if the laundry does not supply enough clean towels or bed sheets. Another less obvious example deals with the output of information from one department to another. For example, engineering cannot replace a defective light switch in a guest room if housekeeping does not report the problem. These examples illustrate the reciprocal and sequential interdependence that exist between individual units within the rooms department.

Effective management under these conditions calls for standardized plans, procedures, schedules, and deadlines. Coordination between units also requires frequent direct communications between executives.

The food and beverage department

The primary function of the food and beverage department is, of course, to provide food and drink to a hotel's guests. In earlier times, when an inn had only one dining room, this was a much simpler task. Today, however, providing food and drink is much more complicated.

The 500-room hotel in this discussion might well have a coffee shop, a gourmet restaurant, a poolside snack bar, room service, two banquet halls, and ten separate function rooms where food and beverage may be served. It might also have a piano bar and lounge, a nightclub, and a lobby bar. This adds up to 19 separate food and beverage outlets, excluding room service! On a busy day (or night) it's likely that each of these outlets will have functions. Often, more than one function will take place in an outlet during a 24-hour period.

There is great diversity in the kinds of activities performed by a food and beverage department and in the skills required within the department. Thus, within the food and beverage department there are a number of functional subunits where tasks are further specialized. To begin with there is the food production, or kitchen, department. In a 500-room hotel this unit is headed by the executive chef, a person of great stature and authority in a first-class hotel.

Under the executive chef are a variety of culinary specialists responsible for different aspects of food preparation. The service of food in a hotel's restaurants is usually the responsibility of a separate department, which, in a large hotel, is headed by an assistant food and beverage director. The food service department is responsible for service in the hotel's restaurants and food outlets.

It contains the individual restaurant and outlet managers, maitre d's, w aiters, waitresses, and bus help. Because of the special problems associated with room service, many large hotels have a separate subunit responsible only for room service. The high value and profit margins associated with alcoholic beverages cause hotels to form a separate department with responsibility over the bars, lounges, service bars, and other alcoholic beverage outlets. Most full-service hotels do considerable convention and catering business.

A convention uses small function rooms for separate meetings, larger rooms for general sessions, and even larger facilities for banquets. Catered events include local parties, wedding receptions, business meetings, and other functions held by local groups. To provide for the unique needs of these customers, hotels often organize separate catering and convention departments that specialize in this kind of business.

Finally, the jobs of cleaning the spaces of the food and beverage department, dish and ware washing, and general food and beverage expediting are often assigned to a separate subunit known as the stewarding department.

Sales and marketing

This department is quite small, thus making intradepartmental coordination much easier. Also, the department is removed from most day-to-day operational problems faced by other departments. Still, there is a division of work among sales managers based usually on the types of customers a hotel is attempting to attract. Individual sales managers often specialize in corporate accounts, conventions, or tour and travel markets.

Also, sales managers are sometimes further subdivided along geographical lines such as regional or national accounts. Still, the sales staff, even for a 1,000-room hotel, usually does not exceed a dozen or so. Sales managers work more or less independently in their particular market segments. Thus, problems of intradepartmental interdependence are usually not severe.

Personnel

A hotel's personnel department is a staff organization set up to handle a specialized function. It serves no customers, books no business, and prepares no meals, yet it plays a vital role in a hotel's efficient operation.

The personnel department is subdivided into three subfunctions: employee recruitment, benefits administration, and training. The personnel director is expected to be an expert on labour law and to advise managers in other departments. While these three subfunctions are related to each other, there are not many problems of interdependence. Instead, the personnel department's major challenge occurs as it attempts to interact with other hotel departments.

Personnel may recruit, interview, and screen prospective employees, but final hiring authority resides in the line departments. The same is true of promotion and disciplinary decisions, where the personnel department's input is only advisory. As a staff department, personnel's effectiveness is largely dependent on its manager's ability to form effective working relationships with other departments.

Accounting

The accounting department often combines both staff and line functions. Its traditional role is recording financial transactions, preparing and interpreting financial statements, and providing management with timely reports of operating results.

Responsibilities also include payroll preparation, accounts receivable, and accounts payable. These functions are the responsibility of the assistant controller for finance. There is, however, another dimension to the accounting department that deals with various aspects of hotel operations, cost accounting, and cost control throughout the hotel. This aspect often results in the department being called the controller's department rather than the accounting department. Two areas that are the central concern of accounting control are rooms and food and beverage.

The accounting department's front office cashier keeps track of all charges to guest accounts. The night auditor must reconcile all guest bills with the charges from the various hotel departments. Although these employees work at the front desk and sometimes have direct guest contact, they are members of the accounting department and report to the assistant controller for operations.

The food and beverage controller, along with the food and beverage cashiers working in the accounting department, keep track of the revenues and expenses of the food and beverage department. Food and beverage cashiers report to the assistant controller for operations, and the food and beverage controller reports directly to the hotel controller.

The food and beverage department may be responsible for food preparation and service, but the accounting department is responsible for collecting revenues! The food and beverage controller verifies the accuracy and reasonableness of all food and beverage revenues.

The accounting department is responsible for keeping track of and preparing daily reports on the costs of the food and beverage used in the hotel. In many cases, the accounting department is also responsible for purchasing and storeroom operations. Finally, the director of systems is responsible for designing the accounting and management information systems used throughout the hotel. This discussion demonstrates the accounting department's direct involvement in a number of day-today operational aspects of the hotel.

Two final points about the accounting department. Accounting is responsible for collecting and reporting most of a hotel's operational and financial statistics. It therefore plays an important hotelwide staff role as data provider for decision making and budget preparation.

In addition, the accounting department head has a dual responsibility not only to the hotel's GM but also to the hotel chain's financial vice president or to the hotel's owner. The reason for this dual reporting relationship is to provide the hotel corporation an independent (from the GM) verification of the accuracy of the financial and operating results of the hotel. Thus, unity of command is routinely violated in the case of hotel controllers.

Strength and weaknesses of a functional organization

The reason for organizing a business along functional

lines is to group together employees who perform similar tasks or have similar skills. The strength of a hotel's functional organizational design is the resulting efficiency within individual departments or subunits. Performance of common tasks allows for work specialization, which increases overall productivity.

Since functional departments perform similar tasks, workers will rapidly develop specialized skills and knowledge. Training is easier because of task similarity and the many opportunities for inexperienced workers to learn from experienced workers. This helps new employees quickly learn the skills and behavioural patterns that lead to success.

A functional organization is a logical way to organize work because it fosters efficiency, teamwork, and coordination within departments. However, the functional design's most important strength is also the source of its greatest shortcoming. The success of a hotel is measured by its overall performance, not the performance of one department.

A functional department's strength lies in its ability to focus on its own tasks and activities. Although this is surely important for departmental efficiency, it does not necessarily ensure the overall effectiveness of a hotel. Because they are specialized, it is sometimes difficult for functional departments to fully appreciate the relationship between their performance and the overall performance and goals of the hotel.

All departments must keep hotelwide goals of customer service and profitability in mind rather than focus narrowly on their own concerns.

A method must be found to coordinate the activities of individual departments and to set hotelwide strategies and goals. Left to themselves, it is unlikely that individual departments would be capable of doing this. Specialization at the department and subdepartment levels results in the need for leadership at the top of an organization. Someone above the departments must set the overall strategic course of the hotel, set hotelwide goals, coordinate activities between departments, and arbitrate interdepartmental disputes. A hotel's functional organization demands strong leadership at the top.

While functional departments produce specialists within a narrow skill category, they do not develop executives with broad hotel exposure. Consider the heads of a hotel's marketing and food and beverage departments. These two executives might only have superficial knowledge of each other's speciality. Their education and work experience will likely be so different that either would be at a loss if placed in the other's department.

The director of sales might have a marketing or general business degree and have spent a career in sales-related work. The food and beverage, director, on the other hand, could have a culinary diploma and a hospitality degree, extensive food production and service experience, and little or no sales experience.

One often finds accountants running the controller's office; engineers in charge of engineering and maintenance; individuals with degrees in personnel administration heading the personnel department; and a variety of educational backgrounds among rooms managers.

Managers educated in hotel administration are capable of filling most department head slots. The longer managers stay in one department the more narrowly specialized they become. While a manager may perform well within one department, he or she may be unprepared.when it comes to problems that require a hotelwide knowledge and perspective. Narrow specialization can result in bias, mistrust, and friction between departments unless upper management takes steps to counter this. Individual departments may pursue their own narrow interests rather than broader overall goals and objectives. This is a particular problem for hotels because of the need for close interdepartmental cooperation in providing guest services.

There are numerous possibilities for service breakdowns in hotels. A well-thought-out set of standard operating procedures and systems can decrease the chances of many routine mistakes. Still, because of the amount of reciprocal interdependence that exists between departments, close cooperation is a must. Nowhere is this more important than at the department-head level, where differences in functional specialities are most extreme. The vehicle often used to foster cooperation between functionally specialized departments is the Executive Operating Committee (EOC).

The executive operating committee

The EOC is made up of the GM and other hotel senior executives. There's no magic formula as to whom should be on the EOC, but usually it's those executives who report directly to the GM. Thus, the EOC consists of the most senior members of a hotel's management staff: the heads of the functional departments who report directly to the GM and are responsible for a hotel's major budgetary units. A subgroup of these executives, the GM, rooms manager, sales and marketing director, food and beverage director, and controller, usually produce the hotel's occupancy, revenue, and profit forecasts for each year. This forecast forms the basis for the hotel's overall annual budget, and meeting annual budget goals determines executive bonuses.

The exact duties of an EOC vary from hotel to hotel, and they can be spelled out in detail or left ambiguous. A hotel's EOC could be loosely or highly structured. An important question GMs need to answer is the amount of authority they wish to delegate to the EOC. Depending on the circumstances, one EOC might be structured to make certain group decisions, a second might play a strong though consultative role to the GM, and a third might have a weak or nonexistent decision-making role.

Quite apart from decision making, EOCs play an important communications role within hotels. This occurs by virtue of the fact that EOC members meet regularly to discuss hotel business.

Any time meetings are held, communications take place. Scott and Mitchell identify four functions of communications: (1) to provide information that helps executives in their decision making, (2) to be motivational by fostering a commitment to organizational objectives, (3) to act as a control device by resolving ambiguities regarding the role, responsibilities, and duties of executives, and (4) to afford individuals the opportunity to express their feelings and emotions. It's important to note that all four of these communications functions may take place during meetings.

Meeting frequency, agenda, and the amount of decision making delegated to an EOC will depend on a variety of factors. The more participative the GM's management style, the more likely the EOC will be engaged in joint decision making. Authoritarian GMs will find little need to foster a strong EOC. The greater the need for change within a hotel, the more likely it is that frequent EOC meetings will take place. The less experienced the hotel's department heads, the more helpful frequent EOC meetings will be because they can serve as a learning and training vehicle for inexperienced managers. Under the influence of a skilled GM, the EOC can play an important role. Some of the ways it may be useful are:

— To foster group problem solving and decision making.

— To build a feeling of joint responsibility for overall hotel performance.

— To help instill common attitudes and beliefs among top executives.

— To foster top-down, bottom-up, and horizontal communication.

— To assign duties, assess progress, and control activities.

— To build interdepartmental cooperation.

— To teach, coach, and build a responsive senior executive team.

— To ensure acceptance of priorities and decisions by senior management.

Well-managed hotels address the need for coordination of activities through an elaborate structure of committees and meetings. Just like a hotel's organization chart, these committees and meetings constitute a formal part of a hotel's organizational structure.

A hotel's committee and meeting structure is usually proscribed by the GM. Each group's responsibilities are spelled out (sometimes in great detail), regular meeting schedules are promulgated, and minutes are often taken and distributed to participants and to higher-level executives, including the GM. The committee and meeting structure of a hotel should be a well-thought-out part of a hotel's formal organizational structure. The purpose of the committees and meetings in a hotel is as varied as the hotel. They address a variety of concerns, including daily operations; intradepartmental and interdepartmental issues; hotelwide concerns; and financial, personnel, and marketing issues. Table 1 lists the regularly scheduled meetings for a typical large hotel. While not the meeting schedule for an actual hotel, it could be. It will pay dividends to review this list carefully. The meetings a hotel holds provide clues about what it takes to manage the hotel.

One of the first things to note is the sheer number and diversity of meetings. Surely, one might say that if a hotel were to hold all these meetings there would be little time left over to do any work! In fact, the effective management of hotels requires frequent meetings. They are part of the work of the hotel. Table 1 shows an average of 249 scheduled meetings each year dealing with interdepartmental issues. Also, the GM attends 295 regularly scheduled meetings each year. In many hotels this is literally the case. There is no denying that meetings are time consuming and sometimes unproductive. Still, there doesn't seem to be a better alternative to effectively managing a hotel. One often finds frustrated, dissatisfied executives in hotels where there are too few meetings. These executives complain about not being kept informed of what is going on.

As elementary as it may seem, it is very easy for a hotel to fail to keep its managers and employees adequately informed. This shortcoming can have disastrous consequences with regard to the attitudes and morale of a hotel's staff. A second complaint relates to service breakdowns that occur as a consequence of too few meetings.

Hotels are subject to frequent, usually daily,

changes. Meetings must be scheduled frequently in such an environment or their effectiveness will be lost. Too few meetings result in confusion over a hotel's goals and objectives. People need to know what is important to the hotel. What does it value most? What does it stand for? What constitutes good performance? Since hotels provide many intangible services, a constant effort must be made, at all levels, to provide answers to these questions. Meetings are an effective means of accomplishing this vital management function.

Hotels are businesses that require an extraordinary degree of interdepartmental cooperation in order to provide quality guest service. The functional organizational design used in most hotels fosters efficiencies within each department of a hotel but is weak when it comes to coordination between departments.

One of the organizing strategies employed to overcome this problem is a formal meeting structure that fosters interdepartmental communication and cooperation. Thus, an important part of management's organizing function is to design an effective meetings structure that compensates for and complements a hotel's functionally departmentalized organization.

Theory of interdepartmental conflict in hotels

The prevalence of interdepartmental conflict in hotels seems to be one of the distinctive features of their operation. Despite this, interdepartmental conflict is an area of research that has been somewhat neglected not only in the hospitality industry but throughout management research.

Whereas conflict between employer and employee (vertical conflict) has been the subject of considerable study and analysis, that between employees operating at the same hierarchical level (horizontal conflict) has been largely ignored. The frequency with which hotel and catering operations appear to experience inter-departmental conflicts cannot be adequately explained by concepts of interpersonal differences or merely through a greater understanding of the external environment in which the actors behave.

Horizontal conflicts within hospitality seem to occur irrespective of the external environment of the unit. Hence, there would appear to be something in the nature of the operation or the social environment of the hospitality industry that causes or heightens intergroup differences within it.

Researchers have tended to explain the industry's interdepartmental conflicts within a unitary frame of reference and have placed undue emphasis on ideas of personal difference.

The result is that solutions have largely revolved around the establishment of superordinate goals. The pluralistic approach is seemingly more realistic in accepting that the organization is made up of a multitude of different groupings that may well have different interests and goals.

Only by the adoption of such a stance can any real understanding of interdepartmental conflict in hotels be attained.

This article outlines four possible reasons for the heightened interdepartmental conflicts in the hospitality industry, either in isolation or collectively:

(1) interdependence—the relationship that exists between departments,

(2) environment—the framework within which activities occur,

(3) rewards—the nature of the total payment package,

(4) status and stigma—the perceptions of workers within the industry about themselves and others.

Interdependence

The level of interdependence between departments in many situations is necessarily high if the customer is to receive a satisfactory service. A number of studies have indicated that where there are high perceived levels of interdependence between departments then interdepartmental conflict tends to increase.

Interdependence in hospitality situations in caused by the nature of work flows; the product or service that the customer receives is the outcome of close and often immediate cooperation between two or more departments. Coupled with this, the time requirements for coordination are very short compared with other industries. In fact, they can often be measured in minutes or seconds. The reasons why interdependence causes conflict between departments can be considered in a fourfold manner: autonomy, reciprocity, role conflict, and goal differentiation.

It has been suggested that there is a struggle for autonomy in the workplace, and that there is a fundamental conflict between the desire for independence and the necessity of interdependence. Where this struggle for autonomy is frustrated, then conflict will arise between the parties who are directly concerned. This could be the situation between the kitchen and the restaurant where the waiting staff cannot feel in control of their work because they are dependent on chefs for their raw materials.

Snow further develops this concept in relation to the hospitality industry by suggesting that staff have a desire to be in direct control of their own work, yet in positions of interdependence this is clearly not possible. Thus, they try to exert pressure on those with whom they are interdependent, resulting in conflict. Perceived reciprocity may also be a cause of conflict due to interdependence between the parties. Where it is perceived by one of the sides that the other has acted unfairly or without due concern or a favour has been done but not returned, then there appears the potential basis for a conflict situation. Where levels of interdependence are particularly high, as between the kitchen and the restaurant, then the opportunities for this type of conflict tend to increase. One party may often have to ask "favours" of the other in order to satisfy the guest or meet the internal requirements of the situation.

Goal differentiation between the parties is probably the most important reason cited in the literature to date for interdepartmental conflict in hotels. Bowey, Nailon, and Mars and Nicod all considered interdependence to be a determinant of interdepartmental conflict in restaurants and hotels, as the interdependent parties placed different demands upon the situation. The chef's concern was primarily with quality and that of service staff primarily with speed.

In other situations this might be reversed, but the different objectives of the staff seem to heighten the problems of interdepartmental conflict caused by interdependence and will vary with the nature of the situation. Mars and Nicod suggested that there are likely to be higher levels of conflict in lower classes of establishment where there is a greater differentiation between the waiter's desire for speed and the chef's aspirations for quality than in better classes of establishment, where both parties have a great concern for quality.

Environment

The social environment may also be a cause of conflict. The environment of the hospitality industry has a number of distinctive features that may add to the development of conflict situations; these include the triadic relationship that exists between management, staff, and customer; the speed of operation, causing stress and pressure for the operatives; the styles of leadership used; and the territorial perspectives of the participants. Many staff members face situations in which the demands placed upon them by the customer and those by the situation and their working colleagues conflict. This type of role conflict certainly adds to the stress inherent in the task and to the existing conflict between those departments that have direct contact with the customer and those that do not.

Staff who occupy positions at the interface between the organization and the customer (boundary roles) have been identified as adapting their attitudes and work behaviour to cope with this situation and thereby emphasizing their differences from colleagues in other departments. The perspective taken by Homans of considering groups in terms of their internal and external environments may be of assistance in understanding the effects of the triadic relationship.

The external environment and the predominant features of the triadic relationship are dictated by the nature of the tasks that staff undertake. The task is clearly very different for staff, such as restaurant service workers and receptionists, who come into direct contact with guests than it is for those who have limited guest contact, such as chambermaids and chefs. Each type of staff has very different pressures.

The outcome of this might be a lack of understanding of the roles of those in other departments, which may in turn facilitate increased levels of conflict between them.

The internal environment of the group may well be dictated by the external environment in which it operates, and this provides the answer as to why, for instance, chefs and waiters may perceive themselves to be very different types of people.

Studies on waiting staff have shown them to be highly individualistic in their perspective, yet kitchen staff have the reputation of stronger collectivism. Such differences in group solidarity and the different value systems that emerge may aggravate the conflicts between the parties. Hence, the real source of the conflict may lie in the external environment that the participants face, especially their role in interacting with the customer, rather than in any form of direct relationship between the two groups.

The environment in which staff conduct their activities may be one of stress and pressure. If the working relationship presents a source of stress rather than reward or satisfaction, then this could lead to the staff looking for an outlet for this pressure, the most immediate outlet being those people from other departments with whom they come into contact for resources.

Whyte noted how waiters and waitresses "let off steam" at the hot plate due to the pressure exerted upon them by guests. Although the recipients of these outbursts were the chefs, they were not the direct cause of the problem but merely the people with whom the service staff had the most immediate contact, and they were the most obvious target for the service staff frustrations.

The nature of the hospitality environment at unit level tends to require a multitude of quick decisions to cope with the large number of unplanned and unpredicted situations that arise.

Shamir suggests that the industry is characterized by a desire for rigidity in operations at the corporate level and flexibility in the units. Whereas this would appear to call for an organic form of organization, the industry has been typified by more authoritarian leadership styles and more formalized organization and communication patterns. This style of leadership and organization in a situation that appears to call for a different approach may add to the conflicts faced by the parties.

Staff also develop territories for themselves and may start to perceive themselves as entities that act independently from other parts of the firm. Any intrusion directly or indirectly into their territory may be treated as an invasion and resisted as such. The kitchen and the front desk have very clear physical barriers that divide them from other departments, and chefs have a reputation of building a strong territorial perspective about their place of work.

Yet in the restaurant/kitchen relationship, waiters must come directly to the interface between the two territories, the hot plate, many times within their normal processes of work, making them resistant to the potential "intruder to their territory" and increasing the conflict between the parties. Certainly, the nature of the environment in which tasks are performed and the tasks themselves would seem a key factor in determining the reasons for interdepartmental conflict in hospitality organizations.

Rewards

Rewards may cause conflict between departments

through perceived differences in individual rewards or perceived differences in the distribution of scarce resources. Feelings of deprivation with regard to rewards tend to emerge from a basis of comparison. Whenever one party believes that it is less well off than parties in other departments, a basis for conflict is established. One would expect rewards to be of primary concern to workers in the industry, which it is often viewed as one with a low pay scale. This has not always been found to be the case; Snow and Shamir both speak of the social orientations of workers within the industry.

However, recent research by Kung in Hong Kong into job satisfaction and labour turnover among food service personnel in chain hotel operations suggests that there may be a cultural element that should be considered. The presence of tips as a feature of the industry is likely to lead to distorted perceptions with regard to the earnings of other staff.

In a nonservice organizational setting the reward system is directly responsible for linking the individual with the organization and its goals; in situations where a substantial proportion of the individual's income is not received through the organization, there is no mechanism to link the individual to the organization and its goals. If this is the case for only one set of dependents within a highly interdependent situation, then the basis for potential conflict is formed.

The most typical conflicts occur between departments, one of which is a direct recipient of tips whereas the other is not. Waiters are recipients, chefs nonrecipients; chambermaids are recipients, receptionists nonrecipients. The reason for this could be that tip recipients develop different attitudes from nonrecipients.

For instance, recent research by Shamir found that

tip recipients had a more favourable attitude toward the customers and the management than nonrecipients. Although Shamir does not indicate their relative perceptions of each other, it is clear from his work that the perceptions of their jobs by tip recipients and nonrecipients differs. Snow also noted that perks such as tips had the effect of dividing staff within the organization, with the result that common interests were not realized.

Differences in perceived rewards may be further distorted by the perceived opportunity for fiddles between the various departments. Certainly, as Mars and Mars and Mitchell have pointed out, fiddles are an important part of the total reward package. When one party perceives the opportunity for fiddles as higher within another department, this may be a source of conflict between the two departments.

Scarce resources are quoted by a number of authors as a reason for interdepartmental conflict. In hospitality situations, scarce resources could be considered in terms of personal rewards or departmental resources.

Where there is a struggle for scarce resources between departments and where it is perceived by one of the parties that the distribution of resources has not been equitable, then the likelihood of interdepartmental conflict increases.

If workers do perceive themselves as being employed in a low-pay industry, then perceived differences in reward may be strongly felt and add to conflict that occurs between departments. Rewards may well be seen as a major source of conflict between staff in the hospitality industry.

Status and stigma

The rigid organizational hierarchies of the hospitality

industry and the traditions under which they have grown have led to a very highly differentiated and established status system. This status system develops around the job title that the individual carries.

Some positions carry a particular status within the organization, whereas others, such as that of the kitchen porter, carry a distinct stigma. This is clearly an issue of perception; how members of staff perceive themselves and others within the work situation. If they perceive their positions as being of low status or others of high status, then this may be a cause of conflict between the parties.

As Sofer points out, people behave in the workplace according to their perceptions of reality, and in industrial conflicts a crucial factor is the reality of opposed interests as perceived by the parties. The status system is established through tradition and myth and reinforced through group pressure. Where staff are grouped together around a similar task the tend to develop ideologies that emphasize their distinctive contribution to the organization and that differentiate them from other groups with whom they have contact. Hence, each group may develop its own subculture and values, which may involve negative or indifferent attitudes toward other organizational groups.

Certainly, conflict occurs in hospitality situations when there are differences in belief between the parties. Although the occupational hierarchies that develop may differ somewhat between establishments, there does seem to be some uniformity in the way in which waiters/chefs and housekeeping staff/ receptionists perceive each other. These perceptions appear to be based upon traditionally negative preconceptions and may form a basis for conflict between the departments.

Negative perceptions of perceived status and stigma in hospitality are reinforced by the high percentage of immigrant workers and, in some situations, of female workers employed in the industry. Snow has noted that some groups face more barriers than others to entering higher paid or more prestigious occupations; this seems to apply to female and immigrant labour in particular.

Members of these groups find their range of occupational choice limited to the lowest paid, least skilled work, which would not be considered acceptable to those people who are able to work elsewhere. In many cases these workers may be reluctant entrants, who are forced into the industry through a lack of opportunity elsewhere in the labour market. They will probably enter the industry with a perceived sense of stigma, which may then be reinforced by colleagues, management, and customers. They will be particularly receptive to the opportunity for conflict with other departments, as their involvement with the organization is likely to be low.

There does appear to be a tendency among immigrant groups within the industry to work together and form very cohesive groups based upon nationality, religion, or values/beliefs. This may well be a primary source of conflict where perhaps the waiters are predominantly Spanish and the chefs West Indian.

Whyte also noted that the conflict across the hot plate was in part a sexual conflict, as chefs were male and the waitresses female, and the males tended to believe themselves superior. Service staff are in a subordinate position to the needs of the customer, and it is a part of the adjustment process to accept that role. Where this position is partially refuted, there may be a feeling of role incongruence on the part of the staff member.

Also, service staff are often required to act out two differing roles, one with the customer and one with fellow group members or with staff from other departments. It has been noted that due to this duality of the roles, service staff tend to be very sensitive to threats to their self-image, whether they come from customers or fellow workers.

This sensitivity is likely to enhance the opportunities for conflict situations between departments. Status and stigma perceived by one set of workers with regard to another and reinforced by tradition may well be a contributory factor in ascertaining the reasons for high levels of conflict between departments in the hospitality industry.

Management ineffectiveness

A company's culture is the basis for how things are done in that firm. The culture can be one of cold precision, warm excellence, or sincere bumbling.

Culture usually results both from organizational characteristics and from top management's ability to formulate goals and transmit them to the rest of the company's managers and employees. Properly developed, a corporate culture can be a tool management uses to build product quality and staff productivity. When management misunderstands the effects of corporate culture and allows a "cult of ineffectiveness" to develop, the quality of products and services may suffer.

Missing standards

Lack of agreement on expectations

A lack of consensus on standards generally gives rise to an ineffective corporate culture. No one agrees on what work is to be performed, let alone how well it should be done and what methods are appropriate. Each employee may do it his or her way. One supervisor will apply different standards than others do, and those standards may even change from day to day. Because top management has not set up a method for achieving consensus on what should be happening in operations and service delivery, a multitude of standards may exist for each job. As a result, the product is inconsistent, guests are confused (or displeased), and managers and employees are dissatisfied.

Inconsistent delivery of products and services. Inconsistency is probably the most frequent cause of problems in assuring service quality. When an entree is prepared differently by each cook, when one room has enough towels while the next one doesn't, when one front desk clerk is warm and the next is abrupt, the guest will be dissatisfied. The hotel or restaurant will seem like an entirely different one on each visit, depending on which set of standards the guest experiences. When guests don't know what to expect from a hotel or restaurant, they often just stay away.

Measuring and managing quality. If there is no consensus on standards, it follows that they can not be measured. Yet measuring employees' conformity to standards is a critical management task. This function typically involves coaching, discipline, team building, and documenting and evaluating performance.

Departments concerned with personnel and service management are generally those where measurement is particularly lacking. This is a result of the low priority given by senior management to these areas, the absence of clearly developed goals, and the inability to delegate responsibilities.

In particular, many managers dismiss the idea of measuring quality by reporting the commonly shared idea that "you can't measure service because it's intangible." Service is a real social event between the employee and the guest. Its quality can be observed and documented through guest focus groups and guest feedback.

Evaluation based on activity, not results. How often are employees rewarded for looking busy, regardless of what results they achieve with all their activity? In both the management suite and the front desk, performance is often evaluated in terms of "sweat on the brow," "bean counting," or simple appearance. In such cases, the quality of the work performed is not as important an evaluation criterion as the number of hours worked or the number of crises encountered. The goal of guest service is obscured when promotions, recognition, and compensation are not the result of meeting agreed-upon standards. Instead, corporate games and a good appearance—down to the right colour tie—can be more important to getting ahead than, say, achieving a low turnover rate among employees or having high guest satisfaction.

Unbalanced accountability

Accounting procedures for some parts of a hospitality operation are more sophisticated than others. For good reason, financial accounting is highly developed, while the accounting procedures for measuring the effectiveness of managers and supervisors in overseeing employees and the services they deliver are less precise. Without effective controls, however, the "people" area can become ineffective. If management does not place a priority on maintaining some kind of accounting system for human resources and social quality, the likely results are employee turnover, inconsistent product quality, damage to equipment, and lower productivity.

Ineffective communications

Broken or misunderstood communications cause problems wherever they occur, but the problem of faulty communications is more subtle than mere misunderstanding.

Many organizations suffer from one-way communications—namely, from the top down. Ideas and responses from employees are seldom sought, and comments from guests are not appreciated. Neither group's comments is considered in management decision making. Such top-down communications engender a cult of ineffectiveness, just as surely as misunderstood communications or poor communications skills.

Symptoms

The cult of ineffectiveness places great emphasis on remedies for symptoms rather than on delving for underlying problems. On superficial inspection many operational and guest service problems seem simple. If a waiter is rude, he must be told to be pleasant. This is like treating a fracture with a Band-Aid; the solution does not get at the underlying cause of the problem. In fact, the waiter's rudeness may have less to do with the individual waiter and more to do with inappropriate selection and training or poor management practices. In problem solving, symptoms must be used as clues for discovering the real problem.

Lack of recognition

Praise is an important part of managerial feedback. It costs nothing, and it does wonders for employee morale. Yet many employees never hear from their manager unless there is a problem. Indeed, most managers must honestly admit that they rarely bother to let employees know when a job has been done well. Employees should not automatically have a sinking feeling when the manager wants to talk to them.

Absence of teamwork

Many corporate cultures reward competition among company employees. Some businesses actually encourage conflict and one-upmanship. When employees are rewarded for taking individual action, the development of teams can be thwarted. Yet a busy front desk, a crowded dining room, and a driveup window at lunchtime demand that hotel and restaurant employees work as a team to deliver prompt and satisfactory guest service.

The development of a team of employees also prevents a department or unit from collapsing when a talented manager or supervisor is promoted or leaves. If the cult of ineffectiveness has allowed the supervisor to set all standards, then the departure of that supervisor could leave the unit with no bearings. A successful company would have a management system of standards that would not change as supervisors come and go.

Trailing

Trailing is the most common means used by managers for training new staff members. In this method, a new hire trails an experienced employee to learn how the job is done. This practice transfers one of the most important managerial responsibilities to a line employee.

The new hire learns the operation's policies as they are understood by the experienced employee, who may not have a clear view of the company's objectives. Any time a manager might save this way is soon lost in correcting problems created by the practice. Moreover, even when training is handled by managers, it is seldom based on clearly stated job standards or founded on basic competency. To do the job right the first time, employees must be given the skills and knowledge necessary to meet a company's performance standards.

Sink-or-swim management

Management trainees are also victimized by a form of on-the-job training—but they often don't have even the luxury of another manager to observe. Managers and supervisors are often expected to sink or swim as they are introduced to new responsibilities. Line employees particularly face this situation when their outstanding performance wins them a promotion.

Recriminations

Rather than treat a guest complaint or other product problem as an opportunity to improve the operation, complaints are often occasions for blame, defensiveness, and finger pointing. Part of the problem is that people don't like to admit direct responsibility for making a mess of a job, preferring instead to sweep problems under the rug. But management also has a duty to limit problems in the first place by establishing a complete understanding of how each job should be done. When management has laid this foundation, problems can be identified and solutions found without unnecessary recriminations.

Effectiveness

Many hospitality managers fail to recognize the difference between effectiveness and efficiency. Merely completing a job ahead of a deadline is not sufficient to ensure excellence. The work must be done on time, of course, but the effort must result in achievement of established standards. The definition of "getting the job done" should include delivering the product or service right on the first try.

An organization is more than the sum of all its operations and departments. It also includes a culture that influences much of what occurs in the business. This culture is shaped—intentionally or accidentally—by the actions of the company's top managers. This informal social organization affects all levels of the company, and it strongly influences the company's ability to deliver its products and services to the customer. Rather than allow a cult of ineffectiveness to grow, top managers should consciously promote a culture emphasizing consistency, productivity, and participation at all levels in problem solving and achieving consensus on standards.

2

Hotel Operations

As a hotel department, accounting is far more important to management success than the articles included here would suggest. In the hierarchy of most major hotel firms, the chief accountant, or controller, as this manager is more often called, ranks among the top two or three decision makers. The importance of this job is suggested by the observation that many traditional hotel departments have been reorganized so major functions now report to the controller's office. The prime example of this is the front office, where previously the front office manager supervised the activities of the night audit staff, cashiers, and other front desk clerks.

Increasingly, hotel firms are transferring the responsibility for night audits and cashiers to the accounting office, with the ultimate responsibility for these information-gathering and controlling functions resting with the hotel controller. Another increasingly important department in the hotel is one that coordinates and supervises all the electronic data processing (EDP) or management information systems (MIS).

In many instances, EDP and MIS functions are now also the responsibility of the hotel controller. This recognizes the training and the ability of hotel controllers to provide for the structured accumulation, storage, and reporting of data in forms that are most useful to the operating departments and other executives of the hotel.

The success of hotel firms in the modern era will depend on how well they manage, control, and utilize the information that is available to them for their own operations. Managers also need to develop other sources of information in the business environment that affect their regulatory structure and their competition.

The hotel controller

The 1989 survey on hotel controller was based on a questionnaire mailed to 750 members of the International Association of Hospitality Accountants (IAHA) who were identified as working in hotel accounting positions. We received a total of 319 responses, representing a response rate of 42.5 percent.

More than 90 percent of the controllers who responded have at least an associate's degree and nearly 20 percent have at least a master's degree. Those findings are similar to those of the 1983 study. The areas of study that our respondents pursued while in college are also similar to those identified in 1983, with over 50 percent having concentrated on accounting.

A significant change, however, was the increase in the number of individuals who were enrolled in hospitality management programs. In 1983, a mere 8 percent of the controllers listed "hotel/ restaurant administration" as their college major, while in the current survey that number more than doubled, to over 17 percent. Such a dramatic increase may mean that more hospitality program graduates now view the controller's position as a career track or as a steppingstone to top management.

The shift can be viewed also from the demand side—perhaps hotel companies now recognize the value of hospitality management training and operations experience in the controller's position.

In 1989, the most frequently cited areas of knowledge were computers, cash management, and internal controls, each of which was claimed by more than 90 percent of our study sample. As with the 1983 survey, although cash management was considered important by more than 90 percent of the respondents, controllers do not appear to have significant authority over the two critical cash management functions of investing (46.4 percent) and borrowing funds (20.4 percent). More controllers became familiar with taxes and computers between 1983 and 1989. The controllers' knowledge of taxes went from 60 to 75 percent of respondents reporting tax knowledge, and the percentage familiar with computers rose almost 30 percentage points (from 70 percent to 97 percent).

In the latest survey we asked the controllers to grade themselves on two new areas of expertise: Financial Accounting Standards Board (FASB) pronouncements and risk management. Only 18 percent were up to date with the FASB, while 36 percent said "yes" to having knowledge of risk management. Also, "auditing" and "internal control" were listed as separate categories in 1989, whereas they were combined for the 1983 survey.

More than 90 percent of the respondents indicated that they have responsibility for such standard accounting functions as general accounting, receivables, payables, and payroll, a finding virtually identical to that in 1983. Other major areas of responsibility shared by most controllers include night and income audits, cashiers, and food and beverage controls. There are some indications that controllers are becoming increasingly involved with the operational aspects of their hotels. More than 50 percent of the respondents indicated that their responsibilities included purchasing, receiving, and storage (inventory).

The number of respondents responsible for the storage function increased 18 points from 1983 to 1989, going from 34 percent to more than 52 percent, and a purchasing function was claimed by 60 percent of the respondents, which is ten points greater than in 1983. Responsibility for hotel security, the least commonly shared function among the controllers, more than doubled in the last six years, growing from 9 percent in 1983 to almost 22 percent in the current study.

The controllers' role in electronic data processing (EDP) and computer system management grew by leaps and bounds during the 1980s. In 1989, more than 87 percent of the respondents indicated responsibility for the computer systems used for accounting functions. Additionally, 58 percent indicated responsibility for front office and reservations system computers—systems clearly not under the umbrella of traditional accounting functions. In the 1983 study, we asked just one question about responsibility for EDP, and 52 percent of the controllers indicated that they had some responsibility for EDP. It's possible, however, that the 1983 finding is understated due to the vagueness of the question. In any event, it's clear that over the years computer-oriented responsibilities have escalated sharply. That conclusion is certainly consistent with the proliferation of electronic data-processing systems in all aspects of hotel operations.

The majority of controllers reported responsibility of tax returns, cash management, and beverage controls. A substantial percentage (more than 36 percent of the respondents in each case) also indicated responsibility for internal auditors, investments, and risk management.

Our supposition that hotel controllers are increasingly becoming involved with all aspects of hotel operations and, as a result, are viewed as valuable members of the top management team, seems well founded. Further evidence of this professional leap upward is found by looking at the executive committee involvement of controllers.

Overwhelming majorities of controllers are involved with such key management committees as compensation, executive, long-range planning, training, and risk management. By contrast, in the 1983 survey, only 23 percent of the controllers were on compensation committees (versus 75 percent in 1989), and only 41 percent were involved with long-range planning (versus 94 percent in 1989).

There were insufficient salary increments in the questionnaire used for the 1983 study, and that flaw caused some confusion in the results. That problem was rectified in the current study by incorporating a wide range of salary increments—from under $20,000 to over $80,000. The symmetrical distribution of salaries suggests that this time we successfully captured the compensation picture. Our results show that not only have salaries kept pace with inflation over the years, but that the distributions have been skewed significantly upward. For example, the lower increments (under $30,000) include fewer than 12 percent of the 1989 respondents compared to 32 percent in 1983. Similarly, the range of $30,000-$39,900 has dropped from 39 percent to 30 percent. At the same time, the high end has expanded. The top five increments of the 1989 study (salaries greater than $40,000) comprise more than 58 percent of the respondents, which is more than double the figure for the same salary range in 1983 (29 percent). As one might expect, experience and the specific characteristics of a controller's company or hotel affect his or her salary. Here there are no surprises: The higher the controller's position, the higher the median salary; the larger the hotel (whether measured by number of rooms or annual room sales), the higher the median salary; the higher the level of education obtained, the higher the median salary. Such results are very similar to those from the 1983 study.

Bonus points

Typically, salary structures for top management personnel include provisions for bonuses. The number of controllers receiving bonuses in the 1989 study was about seven out of ten, up from slightly more than six out of ten in 1983. The median bonus in 1989 was between 11 and 20 percent of a controller's salary.

While many different factors contribute to whether or not a controller will earn a bonus, the most common basis for issuing a bonus to a controller was whether the enterprise met its profit objectives. That standard affected almost 60 percent of controllers in 1989. Other bonus determining factors may include one or more of the following: meeting sales objectives, increasing profits over those from the previous year, achieving personal objectives, accounts receivable performance, cash flow, employee satisfaction, and corporate profits. The availability of fringe benefits for controllers in the current study is quite similar to the findings of the 1983 study.

Internal auditing

As a company grows and becomes more complex, its owners are no longer able to perform all the managerial tasks necessary to ensure that it is operating properly. There is an increasing need to have independent evaluations of the firm's activities that will provide a review of financial operations, an examination of internal controls, or even an evaluation of the economy, efficiency, and effectiveness of organizational procedures.

The scope of these evaluations frequently extends to nonfinancial aspects of the company such as an appraisal of the degree of compliance by employers and employees with the company's code of ethics or perhaps the organization's compliance with provisions of the Equal Employment Opportunity Act. The multiple needs of most modern -businesses, government, and not-for-profit organizations for those types of independent evaluations have led to the establishment of internal audit functions within their organizational structure. Because of their technical competence in accounting, auditing, and related business fields, internal auditors can and should conduct these independent appraisals.

The Institute of Internal Auditors, the professional association of internal auditors, defines, in its membership materials, internal auditing as "an independent appraisal function established within an organization to examine and evaluate its activities as a service to the organization." This definition requires an explanation of key words, as follows:

1. "Independent" means the audit work is not restricted in regard to its scope, effectiveness of review, or the reporting of findings and conclusions.
2. "Appraisal" includes fact finding, evaluation, and conclusions.
3. "Activities" include both financial and nonfinancial activities of the organization.
4. "Service" means providing assistance to the organization.
5. Lastly, "organization" includes operational personnel, boards of directors and their committees, and stockholders.

Focus of internal auditing

The focus of the internal audit function is control. In fact, the internal audit function is a control designed to appraise the effectiveness of other controls. Internal control has been defined by the American Institute of Certified Public Accountants (AICPA) as "the plan of organization and all of the coordinate methods and measures within a business to safeguard its assets, check the accuracy and reliability of its accounting data, promote operational efficiency and encourage adherence to prescribed managerial policies".

The controls used to safeguard an organization's assets, such as locks to secure assets, restricting access to certain assets, and checking the accuracy and reliability of its accounting data by, for instance, review of the bank reconciliation, are referred to as accounting controls. Historically, internal auditors have focused their attention on these activities.

The objectives of promoting operating efficiency and encouraging adherence to prescribed managerial policies have been referred to as administrative controls. Internal auditing over the past several years has been expanded to include the evaluation of administrative controls. In other words, a business uses an internal auditor not only to determine that credit sales and subsequent cash received are recorded properly and cash is properly "secured" but to determine if the operations resulting in sales are efficient and in compliance with the pertinent laws. The role of the internal auditor has been enlarged due to the expanding oversight of various government agencies and the passage of new laws. Today's hospitality firm has to satisfy many different agencies at all levels of government.

The business is required to comply with complex regulations issued by taxing authorities, health and safety authorities, fair trade administrators, equal rights and affirmative action units, pension plan agencies, to name a few, while meeting a host of provisions regarding licensing of activities and the conduct of business operations.

Functional role of the internal auditor

The question often arises as to how an internal audit staff can conduct audits that require such a wide range of knowledge in so many different areas. The principal reasons that professional auditors can successfully do this are:

1. Highly qualified personnel, professionally designated as CPAs (certified public accountants), CIAs (certified internal auditors), and CMAs (certified management accountants), comprise a significant portion of the staffs of successful internal audit departments. Auditors maintain and improve their competence through continuing education programs.

2. Many internal audit departments utilize a team concept in building their staffs. This concept includes persons from various academic disciplines (accounting, auditing, finance, computer sciences, management, marketing, and others) who provide a synergistic effect.

3. Consultants or specialists are employed as needed to supply additional technical assistance.

4. Internal auditors are highly trained to use standards (desirable benchmarks) against which they compare actual organizational performance.

The internal auditor is not part of the operations team. Even though it may seem to be more efficient to use internal auditors to determine account number assignments or to decide when an expenditure should be capitalized, internal auditors must maintain their independence if they are to serve as appraisers of operating activities. Secondly, the internal auditor has a staff assignment rather than a line position. Line managers have the responsibility for operations, and this should not be shifted to the internal auditor.

The findings and recommendations of the internal auditor are advisory and should be implemented by line personnel based on their merits to the operation as determined by the line personnel. In order for the internal auditing function to be independent, that is, properly detached from operations and the functional staff groups such as accounting, finance, and marketing, the internal auditors often answer to the top management such as the chief financial officer, the operating executive, or even the audit committee of the board of directors.

Recent research on internal auditors in major lodging chains revealed that:

1. 19.4 percent reported to the controller.
2. 32.3 percent reported to the senior financial officers.
3. 16.1 percent reported to a corporate executive and the board.
4. 6.5 percent reported to the board.
5. 32 percent reported to the audit committee of the board.

The independence (ability to make objective audit decisions unaffected by influence from the activity audited) of internal auditors is affected primarily by two things: (1) the organizational level to which the auditor reports, and (2) the professional training and mindset of objectivity of the internal auditor.

Internal auditing activities

Internal auditing activities may be divided into four broad categories by the financial and managerial data each examines. The four major activities are:

1. Checking compliance with internal controls and procedures.

2. Checking compliance with applicable laws and procedures.
3. Determining whether the firm's resources are being used efficiently.
4. Determining whether the firm's resources are being used effectively.

The internal auditing activities pertaining to internal controls would generally include such procedures as reviewing the bank reconciliation (financial data) and determining that there is adequate separation of duties in the handling of cash transactions (nonfinancial data).

This major activity area received increased emphasis with the passage of the Foreign Corrupt Practices Act of 1977, which mandated that businesses have adequate internal accounting controls. The activities included under checking compliance with applicable laws and procedures also pertain to financial and nonfinancial data. For example, the financial aspect includes the review of the company's federal tax return to determine compliance with the Internal Revenue Code.

A nonfinancial aspect is determining whether the food and beverage operation is in compliance with, local health department regulations. The internal auditing activities oriented to the efficient use of organizational resources would include conducting analytical reviews of various assets such as accounts receivables and inventories (financial data) and determining the efficiency of the firm's marketing efforts (nonfinancial data). Finally, internal auditing activities evaluating the effective use of the firm's resources would include determining whether the return on investment (ROI) for a property is above the organization's hurdle rate (financial) and determining the effectiveness of community service projects (nonfinancial).

Exhibit 1 illustrates the administrative control model used to exercise control over a typical hospitality operation. Management prescribes operating procedures that lead to actual output or performance by the firm. Management also has the responsibility of adopting standards of performance or output that they believe to be desirable and attainable.

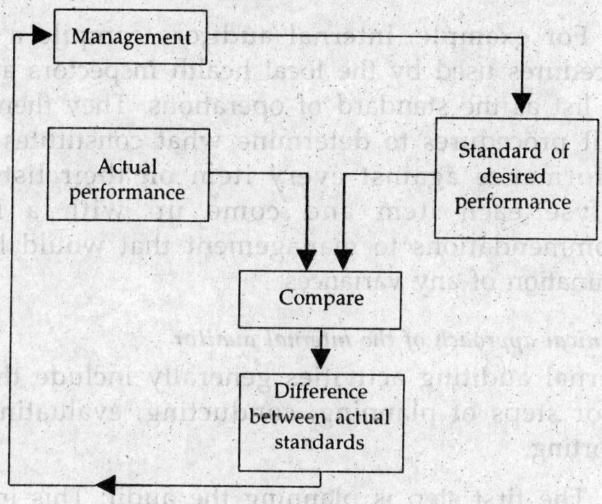

Exhibit 1: Adminidtrative control model

In the model, actual results are compared with the standards and the difference between the two (called a variance) is fed back through managerial performance reports to that level of management capable of controlling the operating procedure. When actual performance exceeds the standard of performance, the variance is called favourable. When the standard exceeds the actual, the variance is unfavourable.

Under normal operating conditions, managers will analyse significant variances to determine if below standard operation exists. They then review operating procedures to determine if changes are required to bring actual operations to the level established by standards.

Occasionally, they may revise standards that are obsolete or in error. Internal auditors use this model to analyse operating efficiency and effectiveness of the organization. They have also learned to apply the model to an extremely wide range of audit situations where what a firm is doing in any function is compared to the desired level (standard) for that function.

For example, internal auditors compile a list of procedures used by the local health inspectors and use this list as the standard of operations. They then apply audit procedures to determine what constitutes actual performance against every item on their list. They analyse each item and come up with a list of recommendations to management that would lead to elimination of any variances.

Technical approach of the internal auditor

Internal auditing activities generally include the four major steps of planning, conducting, evaluating, and reporting.

The first step is planning the audit. This includes gaining knowledge about the operational entity to be reviewed, determining audit objectives, accumulating all pertinent data, conducting an on-site survey, and preparing the audit program. The on-site survey is conducted at the hospitality facility location and includes discussion with the responsible manager and other key personnel and reviewing policies and procedures.

Planning the audit includes detailing the procedures to be followed and delineating the steps to be performed to meet the audit objectives. Though the audit program is prepared prior to conducting the review, new evidence and changes in audit staff may require changes in the audit program as the review progresses. From the planning phase, the internal auditor moves to conducting the audit, sometimes referred to as the verification phase. The actual audit procedures used to obtain the necessary data vary by type of audit.

Common procedures used and an example of each are as follows:

Procedure	*Example*
Comparing	Comparison of actual room sales to budgeted room sales and reviewing explanations for significant differences.
Vouching	Reviewing suppliers' invoices to support amounts recorded as food purchases.
Confirming	Having food purveyors verify the amount of unpaid invoices at the end of the year.
Scanning	Visually reviewing cash register tapes to determine if the number of sales transactions and voided transactions on the restaurant's cash register equals the number of completed or voided server checks for a given time period.
Analysing	A comparison of an operating department's labour costs to its sales for several one-week periods throughout the year.
Inquiring	Obtaining a reasonable explanation from the head of the maintenance department as to why maintenance costs

	exceeded the budget for the month by 15 percent.
Observing	Observing the complete processing of a guest's food order from the recording by the server to delivery of food to the guest to determine the efficiency of the process.
Recomputing	Adding the cost of food inventory items to verify the computer total.

The evaluation phase is critical to drawing conclusions that are the basis for management decisions. The scope of this phase may be best understood by answering these questions.

1. How good is the result presently being achieved? The focus may be how well a procedure has been complied as a measure of efficiency or effectiveness.
2. Why is the result what it is? Related to the first question is the evaluation of why the results are as they are and perhaps why they are not better.
3. Finally, what could be done to achieve better results in the future?

The final phase is reporting the results of the audit. The report summarizes what has been accomplished and makes the results available to executive level management.

The night audit

Hotels have always needed methods for keeping guest accounts up to date and ready for submission when guests check out. Because check-outs usually occur early in the morning it has fallen upon the front office night shift—those people working from 11:00 PM to 7:00 AM—to accumulate all charges and credits guests have accrued and to prepare the bill for presentation. Over the years, the procedure has become known as the night audit, and the individual who performs it as the night auditor. As the size and complexity of hotels increased and the demands on the night auditor grew, the night audit procedure evolved from a relatively simple, handwritten process to the sophisticated electronic systems that even small hotels use today.

Part of the night audit procedure involves compiling the guest bill for presentation. These bills are the accounts receivable to the hotel and must be readied daily since guests might wish to look at their bill or check out at any time. There is, however, more to the night audit than just preparing guest bills. The main task, and the real "audit" portion of the process, is to reconcile all the accounts, ensuring that all charges are correctly posted (assigned) to the proper guest accounts.

Records of each hotel department's charges are forwarded to the night auditor, who compares what has been posted to the guest accounts with what was actually charged in the department. This process culminates in the auditor performing a trial balance of all the different guest accounts, thus ensuring that all accounting transactions relating to these accounts were handled correctly.

The reason that this has to be done nightly is simple. Since guest accounts must be kept current, a "normal" accounts receivable system that bills the individual at the end of a longer period (such as a month) would clearly be inadequate.

Most hotel operations would never consider this kind of billing procedure, because the ex-guests would be spread over a large geographical area, making collection difficult.

Additionally, even a small hotel would accumulate a large number of bills in a relatively short time. For example, a 250-room hotel that was 70 percent occupied during a month with only one person per room would generate 5,250 guestdays of business (250 × 30 × 0.7). If each guest stayed for three days, that would mean there would be 1,750 different bills (5,250/3) to prepare at the end of the month!

The original purpose of the night audit procedure was to ensure that the bills presented to guests were accurate and up to date. The accounts needed to be reconciled before the guest departed.

Since this was usually in the morning, and since the late-night shift at a front desk was usually quiet, it was logical that the procedure that became the night audit would be done at this time. It also allowed someone to post all the accounts that the guest accrued before the guest went to bed, including the charge for the room itself. By midnight, it could be assumed that everyone who was going to check into the hotel had. The accounting day would end with the closing of the last department, usually the lounge, and all charges for the day could be posted.

The history of the night audit procedure can be separated into three main categories: (1) the hand transcript, (2) the machine audit, and (3) the electronic audit. Each of the categories evolved as a necessary response to the increased size and complexity of hotel operations, alongside the development of new technologies to aid the night auditor. While these three categories evolved in the order presented, it should be remembered that there are a number of hotels today that use a hand transcript or machine audit and have, for good reasons, not completely adopted the latest technology.

The hand transcript

In the early days of hotels the hand transcript developed from the need for room clerks to account for the increasing number of guests hotels were accommodating. During the nineteenth century, hotels were growing rapidly in size, and it was no longer possible for a landlord or owner to perform all the tasks required as host. Traditionally, the desk of the smaller hotel, if there even was one, would close at night.

However, as the hotels became larger, the need for desk clerks and other employees increased, and the notion of a 24-hour front desk operation arose. Similarly, a need to keep track of guest accounts arose, since more and more establishments were allowing patrons to charge instead of requiring cash up front. It was no longer practical for accounts to be prepared when guests asked for them. Additionally, hoteliers in general were discovering the increased need for control over the monies that were being generated. As a consequence, the concept of the night audit, born out of these conditions, developed.

The original night audit was a handwritten, manually totalled list of guest accounts. On a large sheet of paper, or in a ledger book, individual guest accounts were arranged in rows, while the different departments that a guest could charge in were arranged in columns. After guest charges were accumulated and each individual bill was tabulated, the entries on the bills were transferred to the night audit transcript. Exhibit 1 provides an example of a typical hand transcript.

Both debit (charge) and credit (payment) entries were included. Row totals were calculated as debits minus credits equals amount due. Column totals were calculated and represented the total charges or credits for each department. In this fashion, the auditors would be able to verify each guest's bill by comparing it to the bill as originally created.

More importantly, the auditors could then compare the departmental totals with another set of totals prepared in the individual department.

Any discrepancies would have to be resolved. In essence, this was the true audit part of the night audit-to review the accounts as posted, and make sure they were all done correctly. Unfortunately, several other tasks were asked of the auditors which limited their time and ability to actually "audit" the books. These will be discussed in the next section. What is important is that the basic function of the auditor, and the underlying methodology of how the audit works, has remained essentially unchanged as the audit process has evolved. The primary task of the night audit today is still to review the accounts, and isolate and remedy any mistakes.

The Machine Audit

As electric cash registers became more popular, specialized machines were developed for specialized purposes, one of which was a machine that would perform the mechanical aspects of the night audit. Perhaps the most famous of these were the series of posting machines built by the National Cash Register Company. Almost every front office manager or hotel manager who started a career from the 1930s to the present time has had experience on one or another of these machines.

The advantages of these machines were several. First, they would automatically total the charges or credits for each department, eliminating the need for hand calculations.

Second, the folio that is the permanent guest record could be processed through the machine, providing to the guest (and to the front office personnel) complete information on charges and credits during the guest's stay, including the date of the transaction, the department involved, the amount of the transaction, and the room number the charge was posted to. This "automated" approach eliminated much of the drudgery involved in the bookkeeping aspect of the audit and freed the auditors to spend more time on the audit portion of the job-finding mistakes and correcting them.

Third advantage of the machine was that each individual posting clerk could be controlled by having separate locks on the machine. Therefore, it was easier to monitor the activity at the front desk. This became especially important as hotels grew larger and the posting clerks were made responsible for posting charges to the guest accounts as they were accumulated during the day's operation. The goal was to require the night auditor to post as few charges as possible, thus freeing time to perform the actual audit.

A fourth advantage, and perhaps the most important from the standpoint of the night auditor, was the ability to print out a form referred to as the "D" card. The "D" card, was a special form that automatically totalled the entire day's activity. This gives departmental totals for all debit and credit transactions that were made on the posting machine.

This particular form was printed out while the night auditor was clearing the machine, or "zeroing out" the totals on the posting of the machine, making it ready for the next day's transactions. Obviously, this would only be done when all posting for the day had been completed. The "D" card naturally followed the "A," "B," "C," cards, which were individual shift totals for the posting clerks during the three eight-hour shifts each day. This system allowed for three levels of control to be placed on the employees involved in posting charges. The department cashiers could validate the charges made by the individual clerks in the departments.

The posting clerks could validate any charges coming from the various departments. The night auditor, who could validate the work of the posting clerks, was the only person who could reset the machine. Note, however, that this system did not apply when the night auditor posted accounts as well as verifying them. One other situation arose during the time that the posting/auditing machines developed. To this point all discussion has centered around the charges made by guests -staying at the hotel, or the transient guests. These accounts were grouped together in what came to be known as the transient ledger.

However, another entire category of guests existed: guests who were not currently staying in the hotel but were nevertheless allowed charging privileges. Originally, these individuals would probably have lived in the city where the hotel was and, as a result ' came to be known as city ledger guests. The city ledger accounts were, and still are, very similar to the standard type of accounts found in any retail store since it was easier to bill them than to bill the accounts of transient guests.

Moreover, since the majority of transactions in the hotels remained transient ledger accounts, the night auditor's function was expanded to include these charges as well. This simplified the bookkeeping process by having all charges funnel into one area. In general terms, then, the job of the night auditor would include the following steps:

1. Post any remaining departmental charges to their proper accounts, whether city or transient ledger.
2. Post all room charges, including tax, to their proper accounts.

3. Perform a trial balance of accounts, to ensure all accounts are posted correctly. Make any adjusting entries necessary.
4. Finalize the audit by clearing the machine and setting it for the next day.
5. Prepare any reports that management has requested.

There were problems associated with the machine audits. First, the machines would post to whatever accounts the posting clerks entered in them. This meant that posting to a wrong account, posting the wrong amount, and forgetting to post entirely were still problems. Additionally, since any posting made was now a part of the machine's accumulated total, making changes were not simply a matter of erasing the wrong number and replacing it with the correct one.

The Electronic Audit

The final type of audit, and the type in general usage in most types of hotels today, is the electronic audit. Essentially, this evolutionary trend is an offshoot of the computer revolution. While the machine audits were much more sophisticated and had better controls built in than the hand transcripts, they were no more than specialized adding machines.

While any discussion of the sophistication of the electronic audit would by necessity be outdated the moment it is written, the electronic audit has several advantages over the manual or machine audit that bear mentioning. Even with the machine audit, the job of tracing errors and proving the trial balance still fell on the auditor.

Today, however, computer systems have been designed to "think" in the sense that they can be programmed to search for the posting errors within the system, thus eliminating another need for the auditor to waste time. For example, a computer can be programmed to perform validity checks on accounts, meaning it can verify the accuracy of the postings. Essentially, the number of controls that can be programmed into the computer is unlimited.

Another advantage of the electronic system is that whatever information the auditor needs, as well as any number of reports management might want, can be arrayed in any fashion desired.

Perhaps the most important advantage of the electronic audit to the night auditor is that it allows more time to be spent on other activities. Most systems have commands that will allow the posting of room charges (room rate, room tax, and local telephone) to be done automatically. This in and of itself saves an enormous amount of time since the auditor does not have to post to every folio separately. There are many other ways in which these systems can save time. Perhaps the ultimate example is in the point-of-sale system, where the departmental charges are posted directly from the department cash register onto the guest folio, thus eliminating the need for the intermediary posting clerks.

For example, there are point-of-sale systems in lounges and dining rooms that will transmit any charge made at the location to the central computer, which will automatically post the charge to the indicated account. What these sophisticated systems demand is a different kind of auditor, one who understands the computer process and can perform the audit functions necessary in the electronic data-processing age. There are, of course, still problems associated with computer systems, including the one mentioned above concerning an overkill of reports generated. The problem also remains that accounts can be posted incorrectly. Many of the systems feature built-in safeguards that effectively minimize these human mistakes. One example is the point-of-sale register, which has prices programmed into it, so no pricing errors can be made.

A third problem concerns the fact that electronic machinery does not necessarily produce physical copies of the hotel's records. Thus, if the system should break down and no hard copies had been made, there might be no way to reproduce guest accounts. Worse, they might all be lost. It is extremely important that the operating procedure of the system prevent this catastrophic occurrence. It has happened that front office employees have had to literally knock on guest doors, find out if anyone is staying in the room, and then ask the guest how much his or her bill should be! There is one final caveat to all those who are learning computer, or even machine, night audit systems. Machines fail, and people who are responsible for generating the folios for presentation to the guest will always need to know how to do the job manually should the system go down. Even the most conscientious controller or front desk manager will inevitably face a crisis situation where the system cannot provide the information needed. It is for this reason all employees involved in the preparation of guest folios should know how to accumulate the required information necessary to keep open the flow between guest and hotel.

Hotel Purchasing

"Purchasing" is a term that has a variety of beverage facilities, to housekeeping, or to what meanings to different people. However, as it is generally used in the hospitality industry, it refers to the processes of buying: ascertaining need, locating and selecting suppliers, negotiating prices and terms, and ensuring adequate delivery. In addition, purchasing includes storage, receiving, incoming inspection, and capital goods procurement. Unfortunately for many managers in the hospitality industry, purchasing is often viewed as a supplementary staff activity that simply assures that hospitality organizations have an adequate supply of goods and services.

In fact, purchasing is a lot more than this. It is a key business activity that not only supports day-to-day operations but has a substantial impact on a variety of major business functions ranging from profit making to competitive positioning. The purpose of this article is to provide a broad overview of purchasing as a key business activity for hospitality operations.

Efficient operations

The enhancement of hospitality operations is probably purchasing's most basic contribution. It does this by ensuring that goods and services are purchased in the proper quantity at the proper quality, by making sure that deliveries are on time, and by managing storage in such a way that raw materials provide maximum service.

The department or managers charged with purchasing responsibility make this happen by working with operations managers to ascertain needs, by selecting reliable vendors, and by developing systems to assure a smooth throughput of raw goods in the operation-from the receiving dock to the storeroom, to the food and ever operating department requires these products.

Control

Purchasing exerts a significant influence on both quality and cost control. The quality of capital goods such as furniture, fixtures, and equipment (FF&E) affects both the image and the efficiency of an operation. Through product research and selection, purchasing managers assure that the proper FF&E items are available when they are needed. Similarly, the quality of raw food and beverage material is a key ingredient in the ultimate quality of finished goods. Managers charged with purchasing responsibility do a lot for food and beverage control by ensuring that purchased food and beverage items measure up to the quality specifications and by doing research to determine the necessary quality specifications for new items. Purchasing also exerts a major influence on cost control. For example, the cost of materials, including food, beverage, and supplies, often runs between 35 and 50 percent in food and beverage operations.

The potential for purchasers to save money through prudent and systematic buying is substantial. Hospitality organizations cannot be competitive unless they can deliver products and services to guests at a quality and a price that the guest feels is acceptable. When competition is based on price, as it often is, being able to purchase goods for resale at a lesser price than competitors goes a long way in enhancing competitive position.

Take, for example, a chain restaurant organization that is able to purchase prime ribs on a national contract basis that reduces their portion costs by 50 cents as compared to their competitors. A reduction of 50 cents in cost may mean that the restaurant has the ability to sell that item for as much as $1.25 less than their competitor. This improves their position vis-a-vis their competitors.

Profit

Purchasing influences profit in two very important ways. First, because every dollar saved through prudent and judicious purchasing goes directly toward the bottom line; and secondly, because the effective use of assets ultimately affects a firm's return on investment (ROI). Let's explore the relationship between purchasing savings and bottom-line results. This typical situation illustrates the profit-making potential of wise purchasing. Let's assume that the Sleep-AU-Night Hotel Company has a sales volume of approximately $267 million, of which 30 percent, or approximately $80 million, is contributed by food and beverage sales.

Material costs for food and beverage run about 40 percent on average, and pretax profit margins average around 10 percent, or about $8 million. If management were astute and able to increase sales by $20 million (25 percent), this would represent a $2 million increase on the bottom line (0.10 x 20,000,000 = $2,000,000). However, if purchasing were able to decrease the cost of sales to 37.5 percent, a 2.5 percent decrease, the $2 million saved would go directly to the bottom line and thus equal as much on the bottom line as a 25 percent increase in sales! The following simple formula can be used to determine the sales equivalent of purchasing savings:

$$x = y \div z$$

Where:

x = the additional sales volume required to produce a pretax profit equal to that produced by a purchasing cost reduction

y = the reduction (expressed in dollars) in purchasing cost

z = the firm's pretax profit margin expressed as a decimal

In the preceding example, the equation would look like this:

$$x = \$2{,}000{,}000 - 0.10$$

$$x = \$20{,}000{,}000$$

Thus, it would require a $20 million sales increase to equal the effect of a $2 million cost reduction on the bottom line. While a 5 percent reduction in purchasing costs would be difficult, it is not impossible. Similarly, a 25 percent increase in sales would not be impossible, but it would be a lot more difficult than achieving a 5 percent reduction in costs. The effect of purchasing on ROA is similar, if less dramatic.

To assess an organization's overall performance, it is essential to consider the rate of return produced by all capital invested in the operation. This is called return on investment. While profit margin on sales is important, it is only half the ROI equation. The effective use of the organization's resources is equally important, and the formula for ROA is illustrates why. In accounting terms ROA is equal to the profit margin times the asset turnover rate.

In mathematical terms, this would be expressed as:

$$\text{ROA} = \text{operating income (i.e., profit)} \div \text{total assets}$$

$$\text{ROA} = (\text{operating income - sales}) \times (\text{sales - total assets})$$

As you can see, one half of the equation is devoted to how well managers use assets in relationship to total sales and the other is devoted to how well managers control costs in relationship to sales. Let's use the following example to illustrate: A hospitality organization has operating income of \$1 million on \$10 million in sales, and its total assets are equal to \$9 million. If we plug this into the equation listed above for ROA, the equation would look like this:

$$(\$1{,}000{,}000 \div \$10{,}000{,}000) \times (\$10{,}000{,}000\ \$9{,}000{,}000)$$

$$= 0.11, \text{ or } 11\%\ \text{ROA}$$

Purchasing can influence both the profit side through cost reduction and the asset side through total asset reduction. Let's say that through judicious purchasing we were able to increase operating income to \$1.2 million and to decrease the asset base to $7 million. Let's calculate the effect on ROA:

($1,200,000 ÷ $10,000,000) × ($10,000,000 $7,000,000)

= 0.17, or 17% ROA

Thus the influence of purchasing on ROA is obvious.

The hotel purchasing function

The hotel purchasing function has not changed very much in the past 15 years. Up until the late 1980s various tax advantages were the primary reason for the construction of U.S. hotels. Providing a substantial return on investment was not expected or required.. In our current economy, expectations on hotel profitability have changed. Profitability is now required along with maintaining the established level of quality. This has brought about a new interest in the purchasing function and greater importance placed on cost savings. Today, hotel managers realize that true cost savings generated in the purchasing department are dollars that drop directly to the bottom line

Without any associated incremental cost. It is not difficult to generate arbitrary savings; the true challenge is to create cost efficiency utilizing standard specification.

Purchasing for the hotel requires much more that obtaining three bids and circling the lowest price. The true definition of purchasing should be "purchasing the right product, at the right price, at the right time."

The statement sounds extremely simple, but when it is applied to the 1,000 to 2,000 items a hotel purchases, it presents a great challenge for the purchasing manager. The hotel purchasing function supports virtually every department within the property, whether purchasing chemicals for housekeeping or stewarding, office supplies for marketing, computer supplies for accounting, or food and beverage products for the restaurant outlets.

The purchasing manager usually reports to the hotel controller or to the hotel's financial control division.This will change in the future because there is a need for a more operational approach to managing the purchasing function. We need to build a team that is committed to the common goal of servicing our customers.

The reporting structure will begin to shift to operations, with the purchasing manager directly reporting to the general manager or to the executive assistant or operations manager in larger properties. This would help-to promote the philosophy of team building, and purchasing would support and service customers directly rather than acting as a support to other hotel departments.

With the increasing importance of the purchasing function, the utopian mission of the purchasing manager is to procure products and services cost effectively that will meet or exceed the customer's expectation. It is necessary to continually evaluate product specifications to incorporate new products and technology.

Purchasing organisation

The purchasing department can be organized into three basic areas:

— *Administrative*: This area would consist of pricing, vendor selection, and the purchase of nonstocked items. Nonstocked items are products purchased for immediate use or held in storage in other departments throughout the hotel.

— *Receiving*: There are two categories of receiving: (1) hotel goods, which are placed in storage in the purchasing area, or other items, Which are immediately issued to the requesting department, guest, or group; (2) items that have been shipped to a registered guest or expected guest or group.

— *Issuing*: Product issuing falls into two categories: (1) consumable food and beverage supplies, consisting of all food items and liquor, beer, wine, and mixes held in the purchasing department storerooms; (2) items such as office supplies, printed forms, and linen.

The staffing and segregation of duties vary from hotel to hotel, depending upon the property size and physical layout of the back-of-teh house areas.

Interdepartmental relationships

The purchasing manager develop close working relationships with key managers within the hotel. These relationships should build and demonstrate trust, confidence in judgment, and integrity. Key managers would include the following:

— Hotel general manager

— Executive assistant/operations managing

— Director of food and beverage

— Executive chef

— Director of housekeeping

Interaction between the purchasing manager and all other departments occurs on a regular basis. Verbal interaction is the most frequent either by telephone or in person. With the technological implementation of voice mail and electronic mail the communication process has become more efficient.

Most day-to-day interaction by the purchasing manager would involve some of the following key managers and issues:

— *General manager/executive assistant manager*: Issues relating to quality changes and all discussions regarding capital expenditure, food markets, quality, and availability information.

— *Director of food and beverage*: Unresolved food-purchasing issues and information related to wine, liquor, and beer purchases.

— *Executive chef.* Issues relating to food purchases. This area requires close communications regarding vendor performance, various size and physical layout of the back-of-the house areas.

— *Director of housekeeping*: Coordination and purchase of linens, paper goods (toilet paper, facial tissue, paper towels), uniforms, and laundry and cleaning chemicals.

A good purchasing manager bases purchasing decisions on the same criteria for all business decisions-data. No one can be an expert on every product available. This is where purchase specifications come into play. Written specifications must be developed for all key products. These products should also be tested periodically to verify that they meet or exceed specifications.

Purchasing sources

There are many sources of information for identifying producers, processors, and manufacturers. Technical data are also available. Suppliers are the best source of information.

The purchasing manager's day

7:00 AM. Inspect the quality of food and beverage consumables as they are delivered to the hotel. This includes rejecting incorrect or inferior products and then contacting the appropriate vendor(s) to rectify issues or determine another source, if necessary. The average daily purchase cost could vary from a low of $3,000 to a high of $50,000, depending on the size of the property and level of business.

9:00-11:00 AM. Attend daily meeting with the chef and the catering, stewarding, and banquet departments to review upcoming banquet business. Included would be a review of the room setup for each scheduled function, menus, and, most important, the guaranteed attendance numbers.

12:00 Noon. All food and beverage purchases have been received and issued. Inventory is now taken on all items in store to determine the next day's needs. After reviewing the current levels and calculating banquet business requirements, the vendors are selected. Orders are now placed with all suppliers. The number of suppliers could range from 1 to 25.

The rest of the afternoon is spent working on nonconsumable food and beverage purchases, obtaining bids, and following up on outstanding purchase orders overdue for delivery. The average work week for the purchasing manager is 50 to 60 hours and may include weekends. For the most part, normal business hours are usually 7:00 Am to 6:00 Pm, Monday through Friday, and 7:00 Am to noon on Saturday.

Cooperation and interaction

Corporate direction and control varies with each hotel company. As a rule, many hotel companies that manage rather than franchise their properties are more involved in setting policies and procedures. The corporate purchasing function is still viewed with some skepticism, although not as much as in the past. Today, purchasing is not a profit center and is established to benefit managed properties. The idea for the 1990s is to do more with less, and this applies to the corporate level as well as to the individual properties.

The most efficient method of purchasing system wide is targeting where dollars are spent and creating the most cost-efficient way to purchase high-volume items. Corporate hotel purchasing offices are currently working to accomplish this goal.

Hotel purchasing must focus on and utilize resources in the most efficient manner today. In the past, a heavy-handed approach was used to resolve issues with suppliers. As we move toward building partnerships with key vendors today, a teamwork approach provides an environment to build upon the strengths of both the hotel and the vendor. Another key component in business today is communication, both internal within the hotel and external with suppliers. One of our national Suppliers has the capability to link their customer service for placing orders with our domestic properties through a mainframe computer network linked to each property by PCs. Our hotels can place orders directly with the supplier through the network system and receive immediate confirmation. This nationwide system allows both our properties and the corporate office to access pricing, availability, and consumption.

Vital guidelines for property

While that was happening, more positive trends were evolving in hardware, software, and market scope. This article provides a summary of developments in each of those areas.

Hardware

During the past decade, the cost of computers and peripherals (in terms of performance per dollar invested) has dropped an average of more than 20 percent a year, and the trend is likely to continue. The hottest development of 1991 was the arrival of Intel's 486 microchip-An the PMS market. The 486 microprocessor doesn't fit all PMS situations, and not all the PMS packages can use it as a platform for their software.

However, the following real-world example shows what happens in a hotel situation where the 486 does fit:

— Early in 1992, a large, upscale Midwest hotel distributed specific bid specifications for a new PMS. Hardware requirements included 26 display screens and eight printers.

— Hardware cost of the lowest bid for a minicomputer-based system was $151,610. Lowest hardware bid for a LAN-based system was $169,427.

— When the hotel decided that both bids were beyond its budget, it asked the bidder of the UNIX-based minicomputer system to rebid the hardware using two interfaced micros with 386 chips. The hardware cost went down to $105,274.

— On behalf of the hotel, the bidder was later asked to reconfigure the hardware with a 486 based micro, which was then tested to be sure that capacity and response times were at least equal to the previous bids. The cost of the 486 based hardware configuration was $68,585. That is a remarkable difference.

The switch from mini-computer to two 386s, and then to a 486-based hardware configuration, resulted in a PMS installation that uses the same supplier's software at less than half the original hardware price. The continuing cost reduction in microcomputer hardware is very good for hotel budgets, but it is beginning to intrude on the market base of the major minicomputer and mainframe manufacturers. It's also actually hurting many of the PMS suppliers, because their revenue stream is dependent on a percentage of the hardware price.

When hardware costs keep falling and the commission percentage remains the same, that means fewer revenue dollars for the PMS supplier. That downward trend in hardware prices is not likely to stop. For example, Intel is planning to introduce a 100-MHz version of its 486 chip in 1993, and its design engineers have already begun work on developing the next generation microchip. It will be a 64-bit reduced instruction set cómputing (RISC) microchip.

New software tools

For the properties it manages, Sheraton Corporation recently decided to standardize on the new UNIX-based PMS software developed by ECI Computer. It was then able to evaluate computer bids from several manufacturers before selecting Hewlett-Packard hardware for those properties. That portability wasn't always available, and that is one of the many key changes in software design that have been gaining importance during the past year. To understand the change in software tools, let's go back 20 years, when EECO (now ECI) pioneered the first successful PMS installation at the Dorado Beach Hotel in Puerto Rico.

The system was functional (but costly) and was based on proprietary components (hardware and software). Until the 1980s, any PMS developer had to decide which hardware would be used (Burroughs, DEC, Data General, Honeywell, IBM, NCR) and then develop the application using that hardware platform's proprietary operating system. As a result, the PMS developer was locked into specific (and limited) tools. In turn, the hotel's PMS was limited in growth and flexibility, and it could be run on only one brand of computer.

Lodgistix's first product used the &M Series/I. Computerized Lodging Systems chose MAI/ Basic Four. Encore Lodging Systems opted for DEC equipment. Hotel Information Systems developed the first PMS on the now long-defunct IBM System/32. EECO used a Data General processor as its base and manufactured the remaining hardware. The operating systems associated with those hardware choices had names like EDX, BOSS, TSC + RTH, SSP, and GCOS.

Other important new software tools are relational database management systems and fourth-generation languages. They have these advantages for the hotel PMS user:

— Software development, enhancement, and problem-solving time have been cut to less than half that needed with previous software tools. This means savings that can be passed on to the hotel in terms of competitive pricing and faster response to requests for software modification.

— In the past, if a change was made to a hotel PMS's data base, all the programs affected by the data base had to be recompiled.

For example, if the system had ten programs that used the reservations data base, all ten programs had to be modified and recompiled. This was time consuming and prone to errors. With today's program-development tools, the same scenario involves only one program change, and state-of-the-art software does all the rest.

Market scope

The classified pages of U.S. telephone directories list 73,068 hotels and motels; however, most of them were traditionally considered to be much too small to cost-justify a property management system. At the beginning of the 1980s, no more than 400 lodging properties could possibly install one, but the steady hardware cost reductions have kept increasing the size of the potential market.

3

Housekeeping and Security

Housekeeping, which is one of the most labour-intensive functions and largest cost-centers in the hotel, is very important. However, it is neither universally understood nor respected by the bulk of the hotel's department managers, employees, and, to a large extent, guests and clients. There are some encouraging signs, however, that this situation is swiftly changing.

Some hotel companies are experimenting with taking housekeeping out or the rooms division and making it a staff function, with the director of housekeeping reporting directly to the general manager. Others are combining housekeeping and other property-management functions such as maintenance and engineering. One study found over 60 percent of the housekeeping managers responding were college graduates and over 40 percent were male. This tends to refute the traditional stereotype of the director of housekeeping as a female who has worked her way up through the ranks of the housekeeping hierarchy.

Information on hotel housekeeping administration has traditionally been organized around models as set forth in textbooks that date back to the 1951 treatment of hospital housekeeping by LaBelle and Barton. Brigham focused her analysis of the structure of the housekeeping functions and responsibilities on the small hotel. Tucker and Schneider, Schneider and Tucker, and Martin have provided a comprehensive inventory of the theoretical constructs, responsibilities, relationships, and techniques important to the modern housekeeper in a range of operational situations.

These works present information in a structure similar to that used in Holiday Inn University's housekeeping curriculum, which says the housekeeper administers "four major areas of responsibility."

1. Management of people, equipment, and supplies.
2. Preservation of building finishes, fabrics, and furnishings.
3. Controlling costs.
4. Keeping records.

In analysing the differences between the "folklore and fact" of the manager's job, Mintzberg concluded that there were substantial differences between what the popular or academic notion of managers' jobs entailed and what managers actually did.

The research mentioned above grew out of similar curiosities: what is the relationship between all that has been written about housekeeping and what housekeeping directors themselves deem important.

A survey was sent to a national sample of housekeeping executives asking them to rate, on a scale of 1 to 5, the importance of 100 theoretical constructs common to the housekeeping literature. Statistical procedures grouped the housekeepers' responses into eight groupings. While the traditional responsibilities of records, costs, supplies, and furnishings were still important, the issues central to the management of people were of overwhelming importance. Specifically highlighted were the following:

— Leadership

— Communication

— Strategic planning

— Hotel organizational interactions

— Departmental management

— Training

The authors concluded that new arrangements of traditional knowledge, constructs, and tactics such as those explored in their model may present future managers with windows of operational, educational, or marketing opportunity to improve competitive position or streamline the transfer of knowledge. The dissemination of this knowledge in the most efficient and effective manner is also important, for, as Mintzberg points out, "the manager is challenged to find systematic ways to share his privileged knowledge." Since 1985 there has still been very little if any analytic empirical research done on operational aspects of housekeeping and other labour-intensive hotel departments. Until such a time as there is, there will be little forward movement in the "theory" of housekeeping. There is, though, no lack of inspirational practical experimentation on the part of housekeeping managers.

Housekeeping organizations

Hospitality is the cordial and generous reception and entertainment of guests or strangers, either socially or commercially. From this definition we get the feeling of the open house and the host with open arms; of a place in which people can be cared for. Regardless of the reasons people go to a home away from home, there is the presumption that they will need to be cared for. They will need a clean and comfortable place to rest or sleep, food service, an area for socializing and meeting other people, access to stores and shops, and secure surroundings. Americans have often been described as a people on the move, a mobile society. Even as our country expanded we required bed and board. Travellers in the early 1700s found a hospitality similar to that in countries of their origin, even though these new accommodations might have been in roadhouses, missions, or private homes, and the housekeeping might have included no more than a bed of straw that was changed weekly.

Facilities in all parts of young America were commensurate with the demands of the travelling public, and early records indicate that a choice was usually available, based on where you might find the best food, overnight protection, and clean facilities. Even though the inns were crude, they were gathering places where you could gather the news of the day, socialize, learn the business of the area, and rest. The business of innkeeping has graduated to become the hotel industry of today, but the main components remain: a clean, comfortable room, access to food and entertainment facilities, and a courteous and concerned staff who mean it when they say, "may we be of service."

Housekeeping departments play a vital role in today's lodging industry. People involved in housekeeping operations service guest rooms, maintain and service public and special areas, and in many instances, operate laundry, recreational, and health facilities.

In addition, the people of housekeeping are a part of the overall team of hosts and hostesses who add their own welcome to hotel guests. They show concern and care when something goes wrong with the guest's visit, and they are quick to initiate action that will make things right again.Major hotel companies have been quick to recognize the value of housekeeping and other service industry workers. Good hotel management does not see housekeeping work as demeaning or menial. To the contrary, all operational management personnel in quality hotels have at one time or another performed housekeeping functions and, as a result, understand the worth and value of those people who perform such functions regularly.

The rooms department

Front desk and housekeeping

The rooms department of a lodging establishment is the department that is directly and solely involved with all aspects of the sale, occupancy, and servicing of guest rooms. It is managed by a person usually called the resident manager. Although the title is somewhat misleading in that it presupposes that the resident manager lives on the premise, most do not. Other titles synonymous with resident manager are rooms manager, rooms director, director of rooms operations, or, simply, hotel manager. The rooms department is usually thought of as a combination of two principal operating departments—the front office and the housekeeping department. The manager in charge of the front office oversees several subdepartments: reservations, front desk, bell staff, PBX, transportation, possibly concierge, and any other form of guest reception function.

The manager in charge of all housekeeping functions is most commonly known as the executive housekeeper. Depending on the size of the hotel, other subdepartments may come within the housekeeping sphere of operations, such as an in-house laundry or recreation department and, in some cases, corporate policy. The person in charge of housekeeping may have any one of a number of different titles, all considered synonymous with executive housekeeper. A few such titles are:

— Housekeeper

— Housekeeping manager

— Director of services

— Director of internal services

— Director of housekeeping operations

For the purposes of this chapter, all such responsibilities will be considered functions of the manager known as the executive housekeeper. At one time most executive housekeepers worked under the direction of the front office manager. They were, in fact, not executives but people who had worked their way up from a maid's position and had little or no training as a manager. Today, however, the size, cost, and complexity of housekeeping operations have put the executive housekeeper on an equal footing with other department managers. As a result, they now have equal responsibility under the resident manager for the operation of rooms departments.

The hotel industry is a highly labour intensive business. There may be more total employees involved in food and beverage operations than in any other area. Also, because of the diversity of such operations (restaurants, lounges, banquet services, and kitchen), there are usually more managers to control the total operation. In housekeeping, however, there is one department head (the executive housekeeper) who is responsible for the largest staff, operating cost-center, and physical area of the property.

Today's modern executive housekeeper must be a trained manager skilled in planning, organizing, staffing, directing, and controlling operations. He or she must also be skilled in employee and human relations, have a superior knowledge in cost controls, and have a strong technical background in purchasing, decorating, and renovation. Last but not least, the executive housekeeper must be an able delegator. Without a strong expertise and inclination to delegate tasks to others, convey the necessary power to act, and, finally, hold others accountable for their actions, the executive housekeeper must personally perform all working functions. And this writer has never found the person yet who could make 3,000 beds in one day.

Housekeeping organizations are as varied as there are types and sizes of hotels. Except for the very small bed and breakfast operations, the trend today is away from the 80-room mom-and-pop hotel. For the purposes of discussing housekeeping organizations, it is appropriate to have as a model a hotel whose size would allow for the greatest variation.

The organization to be discussed would fit any hotel of 200 or more rooms. In most hotels greater or smaller than that number, there would be identical functions, but size would dictate that one person might perform several such functions in the smaller hotel. Obviously, the larger the facility, the greater the need for a big staff, with more individuals to fill each unique function. Consider then, the following hotel:

— Modern suburban corporate transient hotel

— Three hundred fifty rooms

— Two restaurants (one 24 hours and one dinner-hours only)

— Banquet area with 15,000 square feet of meeting space

— Room service

— Kitchen to support all food services

— Main lounge with nightly entertainment

— Banquet beverage service, and service bar outlets for both restaurants and room service

— Outdoor pool, and winter indoor pool with health club facilities, sauna, and steamroom

— Game room (video games, pool, and table tennis)

— In-house laundry for rooms department and banquet linen

— Two company-owned gift shops

— Fully computerized front desk with a property-management system

Hotel organization

Prior to investigating the housekeeping department organization, it is helpful to visualize the organization for the entire hotel.

Executive housekeepers may occupy greater or lesser positions in any organization. Some executive housekeepers might report directly to the general manager; others might hold corporate executive positions; and still others might report to the chief of maintenance. In this case, however, our executive housekeeper occupies the position of a middle manager, a full department head equal to the front office manager and the other principal department heads within the staff. There are two junior managers who will report to the executive housekeeper, the housekeeping manager and the laundry manager. Both the executive housekeeper and front office manager report to the resident manager, who is a member of the property's executive committee. This committee is the top policy-making body for the property under the general manager.

The housekeeping organization

The housekeeping manager is the first assistant to the executive housekeeper and has been placed in direct charge of all guest rooms in the hotel. This emphasizes the delegation that has taken place, the housekeeping manager is not just an assistant to the executive housekeeper but a junior manager with a functional responsibility. There are several ways in which this part of the organization can be managed. The individual room attendants can be scheduled independently or they may be grouped into work teams. In this illustration, team staffing and scheduling provide for a more efficient technique of daily scheduling.

The laundry offers another utilization of a junior manager. In this case, the technical expertise required is more specific. Such expertise would include knowledge of commercial laundry machinery and equipment, knowledge of piecework production, the utilization of chemicals, and their resultant effects on an expensive inventory of linen. Both junior managers and the executive housekeeper have line supervisors who report directly to them. Each supervisor in turn would have one or more hourly workers who report to them. Below the management level, employees are paid by the hour at a given wage as opposed to being on salary.

The organization under the housekeeping manager is incomplete. The number of floor supervisors (or team leaders) needed, along with room attendants and other team members, depends upon the number of rooms each room attendant might be expected to clean in a given eight-hour period. The national standard for rooms cleaned by one room attendant in one eight-hour period varies from 13 to 20 rooms, depending on the market mix of the hotel occupancy. Hotels occupied primarily by travelling or group business transient guests are more efficient to clean since single occupancy prevails and such guests depart their rooms early each day. Also, they tend to leave their rooms in a lesser state of disarray. In such cases, room attendants can clean from 18 to 20 rooms per day.

When there is more double occupancy, such as with families on vacation, access to rooms for cleaning is more difficult and will cut into the efficiency of staffing. In such cases, room attendants will not be able to clean as many rooms in the same eight-hour period.

Staffing and scheduling concerns

In the case of our model hotel of 350 rooms, assume an 18-room workload per day. On any 100 percent occupancy day we would need approximately 20 room attendants to clean all guest rooms. Placing these room attendants in teams of five under one floor supervisor creates a need for four such supervisors. Also, assume that one section housekeeping aide will be assigned to each team to handle corridor cleaning, provide certain services to room attendants during the day, and care for other public areas within the guest room portion of the hotel. Finally, assume that five laundry workers will be needed in the laundry regularly, and that persons hired to relieve room attendants on days off can also fill in for the laundry workers.

The complete organization should now come into focus, except for one remaining concern. Hourly personnel cannot work seven days a week but are usually confined to a five-day work schedule. The following formula can serve to fulfil the entire room-cleaning, laundry, and relief staff requirement. It increases the staff to allow for days off for regular room attendants, laundry workers, floor supervisors, and section housekeeping aides. At 100 percent occupancy on a continuous basis:

Regular staff × seven days =

Total staff × five-day maximum

$$S_1 \times 7 = S_2 \times 5$$

$$S_2 = S_1 \times 7 \div 5$$

For our model hotel, $S_2 = 25 \times 7 \div 5 = 35$ total working staff, all limited to a five-day workweek. The additional ten employees can be organized into two special teams identical in composition to the regular teams and the laundry workforce.

These two teams would be "swing teams," relieving all regular and laundry personnel teams two days a week and having two days off them selves. This portion of the organization can now be scheduled to work by team units rather than as individual workers, which greatly simplifies personnel scheduling.

The functions to be performed by the balance of the housekeeping organization are noted. For purposes of illustration, these functions must be scheduled individually.

Specifically, personnel required for the second shift, persons required to staff the linen room housekeeping communications central, and personnel organized under the senior housekeeping aide for public area cleaning and maintenance round out the total department staff.

The entire housekeeping department staff might then resemble the organization provided in the Staffing Guide, which is a document created to accurately list the need for total personnel. Every position within the department is listed and can be used as a guide to fill vacancies when they occur.

This identification system shows which are regular teams, laundry teams, and swing teams. This particular staffing guide presumes that a 100 percent staff has been hired to support an occupancy averaging 85 percent or more for an extended period of time. Should occupancies be forecast as a lesser amount, a 100 percent staff need not be hired, and staff vacancies can be distributed over the entire team network. Fluctuations in daily occupancy should be dealt with by scheduling down within each team on a fair and equitable basis. This need to schedule down because of daily occupancy can be delegated to the floor supervisor, but controls must be in place to guarantee fairness to all who will lose work due to low occupancy.

Personnel and jobs in the housekeeping department

The basic function and scope of responsibility will be indicated for managers' positions and for hourly jobs; titles and responsibilities will be listed. Where several different names or titles apply to the same function in the hourly structure, each name will be noted.

The executive housekeeper

The executive housekeeper usually assumes complete direction, operational control, and supervision of the housekeeping, laundry, and recreation departments. The scope of responsibility is normally broad to ensure that the incumbent is given the freedom necessary to do the job. This position is now recognized as a step enhancing future career growth. The executive housekeeper is to operate the departments under his or her control in the most efficient manner possible through effective application and enforcement of company policies, the use of methods described in standard operating procedures, and the use of sound management principles. The incumbent is primarily responsible for the cleanliness of guest rooms and public areas assigned to the housekeeping department. The incumbent will accomplish tasks through proper training, motivation, and supervision of all personnel assigned to the housekeeping, laundry, and recreation departments.

The housekeeping manager

In the model organization the housekeeping manager assumes primary responsibility for guest room cleaning and servicing and acts as the primary assistant to the executive housekeeper. Under the direction of the executive housekeeper, the incumbent is responsible for the efficient and orderly management of guest room cleaning, servicing, and the reporting of room status. He or she represents those employees directly involved . room cleaning, and should be directly involved in their work schedules. In doing scheduling, he or she must take into account occupancy in order that costs be kept under control.

The laundry manager

The laundry manager normally assumes primary responsibility for operation of the hotel's in-house commercial laundry. He or she will also act as second assistant to the executive housekeeper. Under direction of the executive housekeeper, the incumbent is responsible for the efficient and orderly management and operation of the hotel laundry. Through the proper use of personnel assigned, the laundry manager will provide clean linen to the house and to the banquet department according to plans and budgets.

Hourly employees

The guest room attendant

The guest room attendant is also known as the GRA, maid, or section housekeeper. The incumbent to this position is primarily responsible for guest room cleaning and servicing. He or she is usually assigned a workload of a designated number of rooms to be cleaned each day. In general, the room attendant performs the same functions in each room assigned. The room attendant will also conduct certain room checks at set times to assist in determining the condition of the house. These conditions include rooms occupied, rooms ready (vacant and ready to rent), and rooms on-change (vacant but not yet serviced, also known as checkouts).

The room attendant will also participate in "general" cleaning (in-depth cleaning) one or more room each day as it is serviced in order to keep quality standards high. Most room attendants work in compliance with standard operating procedures (SOPs), which may specify as many as 60 items that must meet a given standard in each guest room. This is not as foreboding as it may sound, but the SOP system guarantees coverage where necessary. Finally, the room attendant should reload his or her own linen cart at the end of each workday. If the hotel is so organized, the room attendant will be one of several members of a housekeeping team under a floor supervisor.

The section housekeeping aide

The section housekeeping aide was previously called the section houseman. The incumbent to this position works in the guest room portion of the hotel, attending to the regular and daily cleaning of corridors, elevator cabs and landings, stairwells, service areas, floor linen rooms, vending areas, and other special or unique public spaces in the vicinity of the guest rooms.

The section housekeeping aide also provides help to room attendants when associated with a general cleaning, if necessary. He or she will also remove soiled linen and rubbish from room attendant's carts on a regular schedule and will bring supplies from storerooms to floor linen rooms when needed. The section housekeeping aide works at the direction of the floor supervisor, and, when the hotel is so organized, also works as a member of a housekeeping team.

The floor supervisor

The floor supervisor as also sometimes known as the senior housekeeper or inspectress. Floor supervisors are team leaders, having several room attendants and a section housekeeping aide reporting to them. They are assigned to specific divisions of the room section of a property and are responsible for the quality of work performed in the several room sections to which their room attendants are assigned. They also are responsible for the public sectors assigned to their section housekeeping aides. They make inspections and reports and are in all respects supervisors of the persons assigned to their teams. They also assist in the personnel administration of the people assigned to them. The alternative title of inspectress may be a misnomer. Many floor supervisors are inspectresses by virtue of the fact that they also inspect rooms. Other inspectresses do nothing but inspect rooms, reporting directly to the manager on what they observe, but they have no responsibility to correct discrepancies where found because no staff is assigned to them for work purposes.

The senior housekeeping aide

The senior housekeeping aide is a major supervisor in the housekeeping department. He or she is usually placed in charge of all public areas not directly associated with guest rooms. Lobbies, major public corridors, public restrooms, offices, and other areas specifically negotiated as part of the overall housekeeping responsibility are the domain of the senior housekeeping aide. He or she is usually responsible for basic training of section housekeeping aides and for supervision of utility housekeeping aides who might perform specific tasks such as shampooing carpets, washing windows, or project work.

The senior housekeeping aide often assumes responsibility for the storage and accountability of cleaning and guest supply inventories. He or she normally works as a supervisory assistant to the executive housekeeper and performs such other tasks as that person might direct.

The night supervisor

The night supervisor presumes a second shift that has no management regularly assigned to it. This can vary, depending on the size and complexity of night operations.

Other than intermittent visits by housekeeping management, the night supervisor assumes total control of the department after the major room and hotel cleaning for each day have been concluded.

Overseeing one or two night room attendants, a night section housekeeping aide, and several night lobby or public area personnel, the night supervisor is accountable for the balance of services to be performed by the housekeeping department for that day. The night supervisor ensures that all rooms are left cleaned and ready to rent, and that guest requests for service or equipment such as cribs, bedboards, extra linen, and the like are fulfilled.

The night supervisor works closely with the hotel night manager, is usually on a beeper, and makes routine inspections throughout the hotel until the department is secured each evening at the designated time. The night supervisor, like the senior housekeeping aide, is a major supervisor within the department.

The linen room supervisor

The main linen room is actually the hub of housekeeping communication and activity of the hotel. As a result, this physical service area might be better described as "housekeeping central." The linen room supervisor under the executive housekeeper is in charge of main linen room operations.

Maintaining and operating the communication link to the front desk, engineering, and to each guest in need of housekeeping attention are the prime responsibilities associated with the job of the linen room supervisor. In addition, the linen room supervisor is sometimes referred to as the chief status operator for housekeeping.

Keeping up with, changing as necessary, and reporting the status of each guest room's linens needs throughout the day are other major functions of the linen room supervisor. He or she is the prime guest-contact representative. Also, he or she oversees the activities of one or more linen room attendants who perform supply and distribution functions for items such as bed-spreads, blankets, bed pads, and curtains. On the second shift, the night supervisor assumes the responsibilities of the linen room supervisor.

The laundry supervisor

Working as a principal assistant to the laundry manager, the laundry supervisor oversees the activities of the laundry attendants. Normally the laundry supervisor is the head washperson and is in charge of all major wash equipment and chemicals.

The incumbent to this position would also supervise the workload process and production. In our model hotel, when the laundry supervisor and team of laundry attendants are scheduled off, a swing team supervisor would assume the responsibilities of the laundry supervisor and would bring his or her swing team into the laundry. Since there are two swing teams, with each swing team working in the laundry one day each week, this provides the entire department with maximum flexibility and training.

The recreation supervisor

In our model hotel, the recreation supervisor under the direct supervision of the executive housekeeper would assume responsibility for all recreation areas of the hotel. All swimming pool attendants would work for the recreation supervisor and would be fully Red Cross water-safety-instructor-qualified. Pool attendants under the direction of the recreation supervisor would also service the health club, sauna, and game room to provide service to guests, cleanliness, and maintenance of order.

Other employees

Other employees might be found in the housekeeping department, and their title indicates their activity and who they might work for. Almost all positions have titles appropriate to either a male or female employee and are therefore nonsexist. Such positions are as follows:

— Utility housekeeping aide

— Linen room attendant

— Lobby housekeeping aide

— Seamstress

— Laundry attendant

— Housekeeping trainer.

New horizons in housekeeping

The National Executive Housekeeper's Association (NEHA) has long recognized that persons performing housekeeping functions in hospitals, hotels, and nursing homes have similar responsibilities. NEHA draws its membership not only from hotels, retirement centers, and contract cleaning establishments but also from hospitals and nursing homes. Also, the movement of management personnel between these fields is well documented.

When asked how difficult it is for a manger to make the transition from one field to another, a member in hospital service once remarked, "The main function of housekeeping in both areas is to clean rooms and public areas, and to dispose of trash and rubbish. There is only one major difference, however, and that is in hospitals, we know exactly what we are walking into, and in hotels, you don't know what you may be dealing with." That was true—until the advent of the AIDS crisis.

On December 2, 1991, new federal rules issued by OSHA made it mandatory that employers provide to all employees who might come in contact with human blood or other bodily fluids as a result of their job classification with information and training. Employers must comply with federal precautions designed to maintain a safe workplace with regard to bloodborne pathogens.

Specifically, department managers must establish control plans to combat the threat and to provide access for employees to read and understand the OSHA compliance standard. Employees such as housekeeping and laundry personnel, who as a part of their regular duties, may come in contact with bodily fluids such as blood, semen, sputum, vomit, or spent needles that have been discarded in the trash by diabetics or drug users, must be advised of the potential dangers.

Furthermore, they must be trained and tested in how to handle such risks when they occur, and they must be offered the opportunity to be inoculated against the HBV (Hepatitis B) virus at company expense. Records must be kept of all training conducted and of all exposures that occur.

A cost-saving approach to housekeeping

Like many hotel operators, Country Hospitality has had to deal with labour shortages in certain markets. We have dealt successfully with this shortage in our housekeeping department by developing an innovative compensation plan similar to one that the manufacturing industry has relied upon for years. By paying housekeepers by the room cleaned, instead of by the hour, our properties have recorded increased productivity, cost control, and staff retention.

The plan

Most lodging properties pay housekeepers by the hour, but hourly rates do not give employees a strong incentive to achieve maximum productivity. Because the employees are being paid for their time, managers often spend their time monitoring the length of employees' breaks and the time employees spend stocking carts and cleaning rooms. Time that could be spent on training is used to babysit employees. Instead of concentrating on effectiveness (clean rooms), managers must concentrate on employees' activity levels.

Boosting productivity

Productivity improves immediately when housekeepers are paid by the room. The employees quickly recognize that more efficient work means higher wages. With the opportunity to make more money by working more efficiently, many room cleaners increase their productivity.

In our Burnsville Country Inn, housekeepers regularly clean 2.5 to 3 rooms per hour. That figure represents a productivity increase of 25 to 50 percent over our old hourly system. Needless to say, the increased productivity reduced the housekeeping payroll. When the program started, we expected that each housekeeper would clean one room each half hour. To determine the wage per room, we divided our existing hourly wage by two. So, housekeepers who were paid $5.00 per hour were to be paid $2.50 per room.

After observing the actual productivity of 2.5 to 3 rooms per hour, we increased our benchmark productivity level to 2.25 rooms per hour and reduced our per-room payment to $2.22, a cost reduction of 11 percent (but still $5.00 per hour). The housekeepers did not oppose that change because they knew there would be plenty of days when they could beat the productivity benchmark. On weekdays, for instance, the Burnsville property attracts a large number of single business travellers whose rooms are relatively quick to clean.

By paying housekeepers by the room, our managers instantly gained a grip on costs. The system ensures that the hotel achieves its budget targets for the cost per room cleaned, since that amount has been established from the outset. In contrast, the hourly payment system required managers to ensure that housekeepers meet their expected productivity levels so that the hotel could meet its budgeted cost per room cleaned.

Seasonal factors

Paying by the room is particularly effective at hotels with a strong seasonal business. During slow times, managers struggle to give all their housekeepers a full work week. Housekeepers are torn between their responsibility to meet expected productivity guidelines and their desire to generate as many hours and dollars as they can. Rather than try to maximize the number of hours worked, housekeepers under the pay-per-room system will be anxious to get to work, get their rooms cleaned, and go home.

The pay-per-room system also allows managers to reduce the number of full-time housekeepers needed. Since most properties have occupancy peaks and valleys, they often swing from being overstaffed to understaffed, depending on the time of year.

Nothing is more frustrating to managers than recruiting, hiring, and training new employees, only to lay them off or have them quit when there isn't enough work. The employee, too, is frustrated by the lack of hours. Since housekeepers are paid by the room cleaned, managers can challenge and encourage them to clean additional rooms during the high season, thus enabling the property to get by with a smaller staff. The housekeepers make more money during the busy time and do not face the prospect of being laid off.

Beating turnover

This system also reduces turnover and hiring costs. Because they have partial control over how much they earn by working more effectively, our housekeepers are enjoying their work more than before. Turnover at the Burnsville property has declined considerably, and it is attracting better applicants because current employees recommend the hotel to their friends.

Hotel security

It is an unfortunate fact of modern hotel management that simply providing guest comfort, quality food, beverage and lodging services, and a "home away from home" atmosphere is no longer enough. The hotel of today has been severely affected by the many problems presented by the predatory elements of modern society. Thus hotel security departments have the responsibility of protecting guests as well as the hotel's assets from loss. Hotels are usually fairly close-mouthed about their security, its functions, duties, and personnel.

Typically, the modern hotel security department will be organized as a staff function with the director of security reporting directly to top management. We have very little data about the hotel security manager as very little research has been done on that role.

Anecdotally, from the editor's experience, most of the managers recently hired to fulfil this function have come from military security or civilian law enforcement. Typically, the security staff will reflect the nature and size of the threats to a particular hotel as well as the size of the hotel, its location, and its managerial strategy. A director of security will administer the functions of his or her department in the face of two general classes of threats—external and internal.

External threats are generally those that present a risk to the hotel and its guests due to the actions of outsiders. Internal security is a functional area that is concerned with reducing the loss of assets. In most cases, this refers to control of highly attractive and popular consumer goods such as wine, expensive foodstuffs, and, of course, the hotel's cash.

The responsibilities of the security manager generally involve:

— Physical security, which deals with the perimeter of the hotel.

— Adapting policies and procedures to the building design and location.

— Utilization of electronics, modern telecommunications devices, proximity alarms, motion detectors, and closed-circuit TV to enhance the hotel's ability to eliminate threats.

Security directors also have certain administrative responsibilities, dealing with policies, training, education, and human resources, to help the hotel avoid hiring what has become known as the "high-risk" employee. This is due primarily to the increasing risk hotels and other employers face from negligent hiring.

A fundamental aspect of the hotel security director's job, is to develop policies and procedures to manage emergencies. These emergencies can take a number of forms, but in recent years they have included fires, hurricanes, floods, earthquakes, blackouts, robberies, bomb explosions and threats, medical and dental emergencies, and some forms of terrorism.

It is a fact of modern life that the properly managed hotel from a security standpoint in this day and age has to have contingency plans and employee training programs in place to deal with these potential threats. A further responsibility of the security director is liaison with civil authorities. Increasingly, hotels are being held accountable for what they "either knew or should have known" about the realm of potential threats. The best way to keep up on this is to have a good relationship with the local police.

The major responsibility of a modern hotel security director is to assist in the development of policies that guide the implementation of procedures, training, inspection, and reports to assist the hotel in formalizing a structure that links all pertinent parts of the hotel's organization to the concept of total security for the organization, its employees, and its guests.

De facto security standards

Successful management involves being able to predict and control situations, people, or things. If something can be anticipated, managers must have in place policies or procedures with which to deal with the event. From time to time, how ever, despite all attempts to provide a safe and secure environment, something that was not anticipated may cause a guest to experience injury or loss. Increasingly, courts are holding that those acts and events that harm a guest on a hotel's premises can be foreseen and are therefore preventable.

Operators at risk

The duty of innkeepers and restaurateurs to provide safety and security to their guests has been recognized for centuries. English innkeepers, for instance, as early as the fifteenth century had to accommodate any well-comported person who applied to the inn. The rationale for such a rule was that the English countryside was infested with robbers and brigands, and because life itself was chancy except within the confines of an inn. It was established that the innkeeper had an obligation to admit as many such guests as the inn could accommodate. Moreover, first by default and then by decree, the inn and its caretakers became the insurers of the guests' property. To prevent innkeepers from entering into collusion with thieves to steal the property of guests, the innkeeper in common law was made responsible for the loss of a guest's property.

Innkeepers and restaurateurs have never been held to be the insurers of the safety of guests. Rather, the standard of care has been that they owe the guest reasonably safe premises, and that they must take reasonable steps to protect their guests from harm.

Foreseeability

The concept of foreseeability, then, becomes important in the context of prevention and reasonable care. If an establishment's manager *should* be able to foresee danger to any guest, the manager is required to take steps to deal with the danger. That brings into play our current concern with security. As the following cases illustrate, courts have held and are continuing to hold that if criminal activity is foreseeable, reasonable steps must be taken for the protection of guests and diners. This has been the law for decades. Our concern is with the *increase* in criminal activity that necessitates more measures of security for the safety of guests.

Stricter standards

What courts have done in deciding for plaintiffs (guests) in hotel security cases is to interpret common and statute law in ways that suggest de facto managerial security standards. Most of these legal interpretations involve instances where the court felt that had the hotel applied a stricter standard of care to a foreseeable event, the injury or loss would not have occurred.

Generally, such security "deficiencies" involve incidents related to three categories of security standards:

1. Physical, or property-related
2. Personnel, or training-related
3. Administrative, or procedure-related.

Courts find deficiencies

What follows is an analysis of legal cases in which the courts have found deficiencies, and we argue that the remedies of those deficiencies have the potential to become security standards imposed upon hospitality operators by the courts. After a brief discussion of each case, we present data from our survey of security executives in hotel companies that show those officers' reactions to such "new" standards and the extent to which hotel companies have actually paid attention to those standards.

CMSS

In each of the cases we discuss, courts found that inns or restaurants and their managements exhibited some deficiency of care. The courts held that those deficiencies resulted to some degree in a traumatic, injurious experience for the guest—certainly not what the guest expected upon checking in or entering the premises. In deciding for the plaintiffs in these cases and pointing out specific deficiencies of care, the courts have established *court-mandated security standards* (CMSS) for hotels. Because the courts' findings may well be used as the basis for future decisions in cases involving similar circumstances, the decisions are tantamount to a mandate.

4

Hotel Engineering

In the past the chief engineer and his or her department have been relegated to roughly the same position in the hotel's organization that they occupy physically in the hotel—the basement. There are numerous indications that the engineering function is extremely important and can no longer be ignored or treated with any less respect than any other functioning member of management.

The research reported on CEs argues that the position of CE, like that of executive housekeeper, in the modern hotel organization mandates a leader who is now more manager than technician. This person must manage a diverse collection of talents and skills among the engineering staff. This raises the issue of what type of manager such a person should be. This study, conducted on a national sample of hotel CEs, demonstrated that of the range of duties facing a CE in a modern hotel, those rated most important dealt with the management of people, human-related problems, and personnel practices. This represents a significant change from the recent past, when technical duties and activities predominated and accounted for a significant portion of the CE's duties and workday.

The number of employees for whom the CE is responsible varies widely, based mainly on the size of the hotel. One study set the ratio for engineering staff at 3.9

for each 100 rooms. Other factors that can influence the diversity of human-related management for the engineering manager are market niche, sophistication of the building's design and equipment, and corporate philosophy. Therefore, if a 1,000-room hotel has 40 or more people on the engineering staff, all presumably highly trained, qualified, and skilled technical people, it strongly suggests a need for refined people-related skills on the part of the CE.

When Wasmuth and Davis studied the management of employee turnover, they found it to be relatively low in engineering departments in the majority of the hotels studied. They also found that quality of supervision was a key element in maintaining low turnover rates among these engineering departments. The supervisory style that was most successful had as a critical element the talent which "allowed and encouraged [the engineers] to work autonomously".

Allowing the engineering staff to work autonomously pays tribute to both the nature of their various jobs and concern for the human side of management. It also suggests that while some supervisory or management styles may be appropriate in engineering departments, others may not. Managerial style refers to the way that we manage, control, motivate, and otherwise direct our subordinates. It is through the use of the various managerial styles that employees may or may not be encouraged and allowed to work on their own. The extent to which such an atmosphere can be fostered by the manager significantly affects the range of a manager's human-related challenges, turnover being a prime example.

Managerial styles

An unpublished, proprietary study of 49 hotel CEs with one major international hotel company who where attending an annual regional managers meeting sought to determine their managerial style. The self-described CEs were asked to take a standardized managerial-style inventory and fill out a short demographic questionnaire in order to determine what managerial style predominated.

In the inventory instrument primary managerial style was considered to be one of six categories, with a secondary, or backup, style to be one or a combination of the others. The six managerial styles were:

— *Coercive:* The "do it the way I tell you" manager who closely controls subordinates and motivates by threats and discipline.

— *Authoritative:* The "firm but fair" manager who gives subordinates clear direction and motivates by persuasion and feedback on task performance.

— *Affiliative:* The "people first, task second" manager who emphasizes good personal relationships among subordinates and motivates by trying to keep people happy with fringe benefits, security, and social activities.

— *Democratic:* The "participative" manager who encourages subordinate input in decision making and motivates by rewarding team effort.

— *Pacesetting:* The "do it myself" manager who performs many tasks personally, expects subordinates to follow his or her example, and motivates by setting high standards and letting subordinates work on their own.

— *Coaching:* The "developmental" manager who helps and encourages subordinates to improve their performance, and who motivates by providing opportunities for professional development.

A managerial style profile reflects both primary and backup styles. "Primary" is the managerial behaviour one uses most often, is most comfortable with, and to which one normally turns under stress. "Backup" refers to an alternative way of managing that one uses when the primary style is ineffective. Some individuals have more than one primary style and some utilize multiple backups.

Each group is primarily affiliative in style. Restaurant mangers, however, combine their affiliation with a high level of coercion and coaching. This is rather unusual and probably reflects such factors as basic goodwill plus high-pressure situations as well as a predominance of coercive managerial role models in the restaurant industry. Club managers, on the other hand, are very similar to hotel engineers in managerial style. Of the three groups, the engineers appear to be the most affiliative, a trait that flies in the face of their reputation as "crusty curmudgeons."

Affiliative (74th percentile) is indeed the primary style of the group of engineers, with a backup style of democratic (55th percentile). The next highest, pacesetting (46th percentile), may not be a managerial style employed often by most engineers but probably does represent a significant number of engineers who prefer to "do it myself" or work in settings where they find it impossible or difficult to delegate responsibilities. The reliance on the democratic style as backup, combined with the predominant affiliative style would certainly produce an organizational atmosphere where the employees would feel encouraged to be independent and autonomous.

For descriptive purposes, only primary and backup styles are used, but in this case, since neither coercive, authoritative, nor coaching scored extremely low, each being at or near the 40th percentile, the group may be considered fairly well balanced in its ability to employ all of the styles. Keep in mind, however, that the key to effectiveness is not versatility per se, but whether or not one uses the *right* style at the *right* time. The data developed through application of this instrument to this sample of CEs tend to support the theory that successful CEs and their departments should favour management styles that put people first.

At least at this juncture, it appears that the affiliative style works best with people and tasks managed by the CE. This is, however, a small study of a single company and cautions are in order. At this stage of the study of CEs, data such as these can only be suggestive, though they do provide us with a broader view of the facets of management of the modern hotel engineering function.

The hotel engineering function

The functions and duties of the chief engineer, his staff, and the engineering department have been nearly invisible to hotel management and certainly to the hotel guests. Their place in the organization was roughly analogous to their place in the building structure, toward the bottom and basically out of sight. The only times the functions of the engineering department became noticeable were on those unhappy occasions when something went wrong with one of the building's systems and guests and/or management were inconvenienced.

Consequently, in the past, an "out of sight, out of mind" treatment prevailed for the engineering department, and as a result its relative importance was diminished. Also, the personnel of the engineering department were craftspeople and semiskilled workers, usually managed by one of their number who, through longevity and perseverance, worked up through the ranks to supervisor.

Evolutionary stimuli

This department is changing in many of the same ways as other departments of a modern hotel. The reasons for these evolutionary changes are many, but four closely interconnected ones can be highlighted here.

Competition. As more and more hotel organizations seek the business of ever more carefully segmented markets, many competitive features manifest themselves first in the physical plant. These can range from building design, landscaping, elevators, in-room amenities, and facilities to the latest in traditional fixtures and building systems such as plumbing, kitchen equipment, heating, ventilating and air conditioning (HVAC), and the other "behind the scenes" paraphernalia that make up the domain of the chief engineer.

Sophistication. Many of these building systems in today's hotels are interconnected; they are managed in conjunction with other departmental systems and monitored by computerized facilities. This increased sophistication has mandated more knowledgeable management in all departments, but perhaps the most drastic and substantive changes are occurring in engineering.

Return on Investment. Many modern hotel plants were built with investments from a wide range of participants, including the management firm that operates the hotel. These investors expect a certain return on their investment, and thus expect that the hotel company will not only keep the hotel filled with guests but will keep the property in such a state that the guests will return. This also mandates new dimensions to the engineer's job. The combination of increased competition and sophisticated systems makes for more than a traditional "repair and maintenance" approach to providing the engineering support in all areas of the hotel. To provide investors with a return on their money, the hotel must consider the engineering staff a major role player.

Impact of OPEC Oil Embargo, 1973-1974. The cost, use, management, and conservation of energy have added a new dimension to the job of the chief engineer—one that did not exist in pre-1973 operations, simply because energy was so cheap. Buildings were not engineered nor managed specifically to save energy. Since the mid-1970s, most hotels and most modern hotel companies have come to recognize energy as one building expense in which significant savings can be made. If accomplished with care, engineering can provide delivery of hotel services without adverse effects on the guests. We want to avoid, for instance, the extreme circumstances of requesting guests to take short showers while at the same time asking them to pay $180 a night for their room.

The residual effects of the oil embargo are twofold. Hotels that were built prior to 1973 were not constructed to be particularly energy-efficient. Engineers who manage departments in those sorts of hotels have a more difficult job with respect to conserving energy. On the other hand, hotels that were designed and built after 1973-1974 have exhibited increasingly more sophisticated systems to manage and conserve energy without adverse effects on the guests. The first instance represents a managerial problem of "making do" for the engineering manager; the second presents the dilemma of expanding one's knowledge in a rapidly changing technological environment.

In no business system as complex as a hotel is any one mechanical or electronic system the answer. A tremendous amount of attention must be given to training personnel to overcome wasteful energy habits. A classic example is that of the kitchen employees who turn on every appliance in the kitchen at 6:00 AM when maybe only 20 percent are used for the preparation of breakfast and most of the rest are not needed until close to lunch. These represent the sort of wasteful habits that are basically out of the control of the engineer, who is nonetheless obligated to point them out to other department heads. Those sorts of examples in and of themselves suggest further complexities of the engineer's job. Specifically, the engineer now needs to have an active presence as a full member of the management staff and to become adept at interacting with other department managers.

Personnel

Manager of engineering function

Variously referred to as the chief engineer, director of building operations, building superintendent, or some other combination of those terms, this is the individual who is responsible for the management of the building's systems, maintenance, repair, and upkeep. In the past the chief engineers typically were people who had worked their way up through the ranks from either one of the crafts or as an engineer specializing in one of the building systems. They may have been in hotels all their professional careers or come to a hotel company from building engineer positions in organizations as diverse as shipping lines, manufacturing companies, office buildings, universities, or hospitals. New evidence, however, exists that suggests this trend may be changing. The most successful chief engineers of the future will very likely be those whose training and education prepares them to think strategically, to recognize trends.

Other departmental management staff

Depending on the size of the hotel and the extent and sophistication of its engineering functions, the chief engineer may enjoy the services of a staff of administrative people, including assistant managers. These people help carry out the administrative details of operating an increasingly complicated hotel department. Included would also be secretarial support, which may be combined with a clerical function. Among the most important administrative functions of the engineering department are:

— Helping other department heads make purchasing decisions.

— Keeping an inventory of spare parts and building equipment.

— Arranging for the performance of preventive maintenance on all building systems.

— Administering contract services such as pest control, window washing, landscaping, swimming pool maintenance, groundskeeping, and various constr-uction projects,

As the department grows in size and scope, a major administrative function involves scheduling equipment and personnel to accomplish its tasks. That would involve another major series of daily tasks in the administration of an engineering department.

Scheduling may benefit greatly from technological advances such as microcomputers or the hotel's mainframe computer system, but in a building whose systems are as complicated and interrelated as those of a hotel, engineering must be prepared to react to unscheduled events ranging from overflowing toilets to stuck elevators, gas leaks, and so forth.

A final administrative function sets the groundwork for managerial and administrative decisions that affect the long-term operation of the engineering department and, by extension, the hotel itself. That is the keeping of accurate and up-to-date records regarding the various building systems and installation of that capital equipment for which the engineer is responsible.

Those engineers who have the luxury of a well-developed administrative staff find their job in managing the building, its systems, and their attendant problems much easier if complete, accurate, and up-to-date records are available as the basis for planning, purchasing, budgeting, and control. These are the sorts of administrative details that complicate the job of any manager but may be particularly troubling to the engineer.

One of the main reasons for this is that while the engineering department is responsible for the maintenance and repair of sophisticated and complicated building systems, under most circumstances these systems and their components are often operated by a wide range of people ranging from employees to guests. Particularly in the case of guests, engineers have little or no control over the way in which guests treat guest room equipment and fixtures for which they are responsible.

Technical specialists

Heating, ventilating, and air conditioning (HVAC) is concerned with supplying the various production, public, and guest room areas of the hotel with a clean, controlled, and comfortable indoor environment.

Modern building HVAC systems provide for heating or cooling the air, adding or deleting moisture from the air to adjust for optimum relative humidity, filtering or cleaning the air, and moving the air from place to place within the hotel.

The HVAC systems provide for a number of complete changes of air in a room per hour dependent upon local codes and activities within that particular area of the hotel. One of the complicating factors here that challenge the engineering department is that various areas of the hotel have different requirements for air—for instance, requirements differ from the guest room areas to the kitchen area to public areas such as the lobby, bars, restaurants, or housekeeping and laundry facilities. Engineers call this "providing the system with balance," and it is a major function of the individuals who are in charge of the HVAC to deliver the optimum environment to each area of the hotel and to adjust the HVAC system to accomplish this.

The plumbing system in a modern hotel has to perform a number of balancing functions also. First and foremost in the minds of management is the delivery of quality water service to guest room areas. Guests want high-quality water that is free from visual defects such as dirt or rust, does not carry any odours, and tastes clean and fresh. Guests also want water that is hot enough to shave, bathe, and wash without the danger of scalding themselves; and they also want that water in generous supply. Nothing is more frustrating to a hotel guest who is paying over $100 a night for a room to find that the hotel has run out of hot water in the middle of a morning shave or shower.

At the same time, the engineering department is expected to deliver "production" hot and cold water to the kitchen areas, the housekeeping and laundry areas, and the various food service areas. Providing for the delivery of high-quality water service to the various user groups in the hotel is a major part of the engineering function, a function that is only noticed when there is some obvious defect in the delivery of that particular service.

A similar case may be made for the delivery of electricity to the various areas within the hotel. As in providing high-quality plumbing services, the electrical systems of the hotel also have to be designed and maintained to serve various user groups. Again, like plumbing, there is no substitute for the lack of electricity. The engineering staff must provide the hotel with electrical service designed to meet the needs of individual departments as well as the guests.

Refrigeration, food production equipment, and computer systems are examples of other building systems whose repair, maintenance, replacement, and/or management may be the responsibility of the engineering department. While the maintenance of many of these Systems may be contracted to outside agencies, the engineering department nonetheless is the first line of defence in keeping them operating efficiently.

In most modern hotels, the installation and service of elevator systems are generally the province of the elevator manufacturer, and hotels typically have extended maintenance agreements for their elevators.

Most engineering departments will, however, closely monitor the operation of the elevator systems. In modern high-rise hotels with high-speed elevator service, the slightest problem with that service should be quickly identified and reported to the contractors. It is generally the responsibility of the engineering department to monitor these services and their contracts closely and carefully.

Depending upon the size of the hotel and complexity of its services, an engineering department may employ on a full-time basis one or more carpenters and cabinetmakers to maintain, repair, and build fixtures and furniture for the hotel's guests and staff. Similarly, if this service is not contracted out, hotels may employ an upholsterer whose major task is to maintain the high-quality appearance of the vast collection of furniture in a typical hotel. Painting and upkeep of the hotel's grounds and landscaping also represent ongoing functions that require constant attention. These services may be contracted to outside agencies or supplies, but they are included here to suggest the range of functions for which the engineering department is responsible.

Issues

The engineers surveyed were asked to judge the relative importance of each of 58 statements relating to the operation of a modern hotel engineering department. A statistical procedure was applied to rank order the statements in terms of their importance.

Departmental management

The modern hotel engineers deem those activities, which relate to management of their departments, as highly important to success: communicating with employees, providing for a safe environment, being able to organize the various tasks, activities, and personnel in the department, and providing leadership. All this suggests that the foremost issues facing the chief engineer today are those that relate to managerial rather than technical skills, which were traditionally thought to be the chief engineer's main concern.

Energy

The fact that three energy-related items were rated in the top ten issues by all engineers responding suggests that this realm of issues relating to energy has not yet been addressed satisfactorily by the majority of these professionals. It also suggests that energy will continue to be an issue in the foreseeable future.

Relations with top management

Another major dimension of the engineer's job can be seen by the importance the engineers attached to this issue. Of the other departments that the engineers were asked to rank their relationships with, only two, housekeeping and purchasing, ranked within the top 50 percent of these 58 items. Many of the chief engineers contacted for comment agreed with this ranking with top management. They said on a regular basis it is becoming an increasingly important part of their job to not only report to top management but to educate them as to the importance of the engineering function.

Equipment

The more technical aspects of the chief engineer's job have not been ignored by the rankings assigned to these 58 operational statements. That knowledge of maintenance of equipment ranked clearly first among the other statements as well as the knowledge of types of equipment statement in the top ten suggests that while the job of the chief engineer may be evolving toward one of a more managerial nature, some of the traditional technical aspects of the job still play a major role in the daily discharge of an engineer's responsibility.

The engineers themselves say that they are involved more with issues and problems related to people and departmental action and interaction than in the past, when most of the issues and problems they faced on a regular basis involved equipment and systems. It also appears that in the future chief engineers are going to have to be more adept at inter- and intradepartmental politics. To provide the hotel and its guests with high-quality services relative to the physical and environmental systems of the building, the chief engineer is going to have to compete with other department heads for scarce resources related to personnel, technology, and "operating elbow room."

The engineering department, its management, and to a certain extent its staff and technical experts represent an organizational function of the modern hotel that is in the process of evolutionary change. As stated at the outset, this change is driven by 4 number of factors. The future of successful hotel organizations will hinge to a great extent on the ability of hotel managements to recognize the importance of the contributions of the engineering department to the delivery of guest services and thus to maintain a high return on investment for the owners of the property.

The evolution of the hotel engineer's job

Considering the many substantial changes that have recently affected the hotel engineering department, it is not surprising that the chief engineer's position is not always clearly understood by others in the hotel. At one end of the spectrum is the perception of the chief engineer (CE) as an irascible curmudgeon who knows the meaning of every clank in every pipe and who knows where to kick the ice machine, how to relight the boiler, and how to build a pool table, a craps table, or a dining room table (or maybe all three at once) on the same day the request comes in.

On the other end is the picture of the CE as a manager dressed in coat and tie, who is equally comfortable in the executive suite and the boiler room and who commands an array of modern technology only slightly less complicated than the flight deck of the starship *Enterprise.* The energy upheaval of the 1970s was a primary impetus for development of the "new" chief engineer's position.

Borsenik points out that during the prior era of stable utility prices, limited hotel services, and low labour costs, maintenance and engineering functions were related to the minor status of a "necessary evil." In the 1970s, a period of rising energy prices and accelerating technical advances, hotel managements started to recognize the critical role that the CE could play. The problem was that many CEs did not have the management skills to balance their excellent technical abilities.

Most written discussions of the CE's role state that the position now embraces more management-oriented functions, but they do not always specify what those functions involve. In his text on hotel engineering, Aulbach states: The need for effectively managing the engineering maintenance department is just as important as it is for any other department. In addition to specialized technical knowledge, the chief engineer must possess managerial abilities if the department is to attain its goals.

Aulbach adds that the role of the engineering and maintenance department has changed over the years from one of "just keeping things running" to one of management. The CE must also stay abreast of rapid technological developments and meet guest demands that involve changes in the physical plant. In this chapter we will review the events that have forged a new identity for chief engineers and present the results of a survey of how 74 CEs view their jobs.

Forces for change

A variety of new challenges have arisen for the hotel chief engineer. Most have not come through sudden revolutions but rather have developed from a combination of related evolutionary factors. Foremost among these factors is competition.

As more hotel organizations have sought the business of ever more carefully segmented markets, many have added technical improvements to their physical plants that must be maintained by the engineering department. These features can range from general building design to specific in-room facilities (for example, refrigerators) and the latest in traditional fixtures and building systems. The management of these physical assets is fundamental to the CE's job.

Sophistication

Many features and systems in today's hotels are interconnected and managed in conjunction with other departmental systems and monitored by computerized facilities. This increased equipment sophistication means all managers must be more knowledgeable, but the most drastic and substantive changes have been occurring in engineering. As a result, the CE must not only be broadly knowledgeable in the latest equipment and systems, but must also be able to recruit, train, and manage a staff that can meet the challenges of maintaining technologically advanced equipment. The combination of increased market competition and sophisticated systems has greatly expanded the engineer's job. In addition to the traditional "repair and maintenance" functions, the job now involves providing engineering support to all areas of the hotel.

Energy

The cost, use, and conservation of energy have added a new dimension to the job of the chief engineer—one that essentially did not exist before 1973. Because energy was previously so cheap, buildings were neither engineered nor managed specifically to save energy. Since the restructuring of the energy industry in the mid-1970s, most hotels and hotel companies have recognized energy as one area in which significant savings could be achieved. Most energy conservation programs provide for delivery of hotel services without adverse effects on the guest. Hotel managements want to avoid, for instance, the extreme case of a guest being requested to take a short shower in a room that costs upward of $100 per night.

The residual effects of the oil embargo of 1973 are twofold. Hotels that were built prior to 1973 were not constructed to be particularly energy-efficient. Engineers working in those hotels have a difficult job with respect to conserving energy.

On the other hand, many hotels designed and built after this time contain sophisticated systems that conserve energy without affecting guest comfort. The first instance presents the CE with a managerial problem of "making do"; the second requires continual expansion of the chief's technical knowledge.

A mechanical or electronic system can never be the only answer to energy conservation in a business as complex as a hotel. A tremendous amount of attention must be given to training personnel to overcome wasteful habits. Here is a further complication for the CE, because in the case of energy conservation the CE's responsibility extends beyond engineering to all hotel departments.

Theory

Successful CEs should exhibit a blend of technical knowledge and managerial expertise. The discussion further suggests that CEs will be spending a greater percentage of their time on managerial matters, and that these have assumed levels of importance at least as great as the technical aspects of the CE's job.

Like many departments in hotels, engineering is dominated by white males. In part, this phenomenon reflects the traditional difficulty that minorities and women have encountered in moving into the upper management of any hotel department. But the preponderance of white males is more glaring in engineering than in other fields, presumably because the trades and skills of workers and managers in this department are historically not those widely open to minorities and women.

This CE also reported that an increasing number of people with college backgrounds and degrees were joining the engineering department, to the exclusion of those who have followed the more traditional "up-through-the-ranks" path. Since there are no comparative data from other studies of chief engineers, it is difficult to determine whether the trend toward college-educated engineers is growing.

Nearly all the respondents considered their careers to be successful. This assessment was supported by other measures: The CEs said they were continually being recruited for other jobs, and they strongly felt their economic position had improved within the previous five years. That the vast majority of respondents intended to remain in engineering also signals confidence in their ability to contribute to the field. These career satisfaction data compared favourably with the results of a similar survey of hotel general managers.

Second careers

A comparison of the average number of years the CEs had spent in the hospitality industry with their ages indicated that many of them had come to the hotel business from other industries. This was apparently true, however, only of the older CEs. The younger engineers had been in hotel administration for the bulk of their careers.

While the hotels represented in the sample ranged from fairly small (124 rooms) to megahotels (1,800-plus rooms), there was a slight bias toward larger hotels in the respondents. Seventy percent of the respondents were from chain hotels (the sample comprised 55 percent large chain hotels and 45 independents or regional chains), and the average engineering staff size of nearly 26 would also indicate a stronger response from larger operations.

It is possible that one cause for the uneven return is that many chain hotels' engineering departments are managed to be more receptive to research projects such as this one. One international chain, for instance, has requested permission to replicate this study in its own hotels, A corporate officer at another chain said that his firm's changing corporate culture increasingly reflects the potential contributions of the chief engineer, so individuals in the engineering department may be more inclined to participate in such research.

Testing theories

After the engineers judged the relative importance of and time devoted to each of the 58 items in the survey, the statements were ranked according to the importance and time ratings.

Departmental management

Eight of the top 20 items involved management. The respondents' high ranking of such matters as communicating with employees, organizing and providing training, maintaining a safe environment, and providing motivational leadership suggests the importance of managerial skills rather than mere technical knowledge.

Energy

Energy remained a top priority. The fact that five energy-related items were in the top 20 (for example, number 2, energy conservation, and number 3, energy management) indicates that energy is still a problem for most engineers, and that it will continue to be a priority in the foreseeable future.

Management relationships

Another major dimension of the CE's job was relationships with other managers. This was the number 5 item, and it was ranked far above relationships with individual departments. Commenting on this finding, many chief engineers said regular interaction with top management had become a large part of their job. They not only reported to top management but were also responsible for educating top managers about the engineering function. Housekeeping was the most significant department for the engineers, outside of their own. Housekeeping personnel working in all areas of the hotel have become the "eyes and ears" of the engineering manager in monitoring the condition and efficiency of the building's systems and physical assets.

Equipment

Keeping the equipment operating was still the number-one consideration for the chief engineers. Three other equipment-related items were also in the top 20, and it seems clear that no matter how managerial the CE's position becomes, the technical aspects of the job will still be a major concern.

Computers

Most CEs did not rate the items relating to computers because most don't use computers. Yet computer-related items were very important to the CEs who *did* use automated systems.

Time constraints

The amount of time spent on various aspects of the chief engineer's job corresponded closely to the 20 most important aspects of the job. With only one exception, the 20 items rated most important were also on the list of the most time-consuming duties.

Equipment maintenance, for instance, was first on both lists. In this respect, there was a remarkable amount of agreement on the part of the 74 respondents. The congruence of the two lists indicates that these managers have their priorities in order: They are devoting time to the duties they believe are most critical to their department's operations.

There was a consistent relationship between the importance of the duties and the time available to perform them. In every instance, for all 58 factors, the CEs gave a significantly higher rating to the importance of each factor than to the time devoted to it.

Looking again at the number-one item on both lists, the mean importance rating for knowledge of maintenance of equipment was 4.7, while the mean rating of the time devoted to this item was 4.2. One might argue that most managers find they don't have enough time to devote to all their responsibilities, but the CE's job is exceptionally broad and complex.

The responsibility for overseeing a diverse collection of personnel and complex systems and equipment undoubtedly engenders an unusual managerial strain for the chief engineers. For example, one engineer said his ability to devote time to administrative and managerial duties suffered from the need to dispatch numerous immediate problems involving personnel and systems.

With their greater involvement in hotel management, chief engineers will have to be more adept at inter and intradepartmental organizational policies. The CE will have to compete with other department heads for budget resources related to personnel and technology so that guest services can be maintained.

Moving toward management

This study sought to document the current role of the hotel chief engineer. Because this is the first study of its kind, there are no comparative data, and other researchers may be interested in testing other aspects of this topic. Hotel operators can use this information in establishing management structure. Companies may wish to use these data as the basis for comparisons with their own organizations. And engineers may find particular value in comparing operational aspects of their departments and careers to those presented here. If the role and function of the engineering department are indeed changing substantially, hotel companies should document those changes and adjust their policies, personnel, and procedures to take competitive advantage of them.

7
Marketing

For most hotel companies, it was only during the 1980s that the word "marketing" became anything more than a euphemism for sales. Indeed, in the competitive landscape of the not too distant past, most activities that related to putting guests in rooms could be accomplished by an aggressive and knowledgeable sales staff. In today's competitive environment, this has become impossible.

Hotel companies that have designed a sophisticated inventory of hospitality services need a similarly sophisticated scheme for letting their clientele know about their services. For most hotel companies, true marketing has now evolved to reflect their own sophistication as well as that of guests and potential clientele.

Business travellers, travel agents, and meeting planners who represent and book group and convention business are well educated and informed consumers. To serve this clientele, hotels have had to develop marketing efforts and product segmentation to first interest the market and then to allow people in that market to make intelligent choices from among competitors. Marketing is thus an umbrella term that covers a number of strategic and tactical activities designed to tell the clientele the "story" of the hotel's services and to encourage that clientele to make choices based on how one hotel's marketing message compares to alternatives. In any given hotel or hotel company, marketing includes: a range of sales activities; public relations; advertising in all media; design of symbols and images; and, increasingly, the departments of convention services, reservations, and perhaps catering. Research also plays a major role in designing marketing strategies and tactics.

Managers understand the range within which these data may be interpreted and applied. Successful managers and high-quality organizations will always be seeking information and data that allow them to make accurate decisions and design effective marketing and/or managerial efforts. These data can take a number of different forms, but for the most part they deal with the various characteristics of the hotel's target market that affect its choice of hotels. Hotels will find mechanisms to accumulate the following sorts of data about their guests and potential guests:

— *Geographic:* What sorts of communities are represented; what parts of the country or world; how far do they travel.

— *Demographic:* Age, sex, occupation, income, ethnicity, family, education.

— *Psychographic:* Client's self-image; social or peer group; lifestyle; personality traits.

— *Behaviouristic:* Is hotel choice a routine or special occasion; what does guest seek in terms of quality, service, economy; user status (non-user, ex-user, potential user, regular user, first-time user); usage rate (light, medium, heavy); loyalty.

While many of the specific details or programs included under the marketing umbrella can be farmed out to agencies that specialize in advertising or public relations, the hotel's strategic marketing plan has to come from within the hotel organization itself.

If marketing, as it has been said, is the promise, then it is the hotel's employees who keep that promise. This is particularly important with the group market, represented in large part by meeting planners. In the Rutherford and Umbreit study, of the 316 critical incidents gleaned from 52 separate MP interviews, over 100, or 32 percent, had the convention services manager (CSM) as its central focus.

In recognition of the central importance of the CSM in keeping the promise, many hotels include convention services as a functional component of the marketing department.

The professionals in these departments design their activities specifically to make sure that the efforts and promises of the sales department and marketing messages are delivered to the group while it is on the premises of the hotel. Michael Adams's article on "a day in the life" of such a manager provides graphic evidence of the importance of this position. It also gives us a detailed look at the responsibilities that are important for this professional to master in participating in the hosting of such an event.

All in all, the strategies, tactics, activities, personnel and concepts described by articles in this section provide an overview that only hints at the importance of effective management of the marketing function.

Marketing is perhaps the most written-about topic in hospitality literature. Because there is such a diversity of opinion it can be argued that there is no one "right" way to market, nor is there any single piece of literature generally considered seminal to hotel marketing. The reader is urged to consider the references used by contributing authors and the suggested readings, and to actively peruse recent hospitality journals to achieve greater understanding of this fascinating process and, by extension, its management.

We've seen great changes in the travel industry during the 1980s, with mergers, acquisitions, niche marketing, and brand extensions. With all this activity, the consensus is that the travel industry is maturing. While that may be true, there's no likelihood that change will slow down.

On the contrary, we will see tremendous proliferation of travel services and experimental products and services. With the pressure of competition, many of these new products will fail. Companies that are now dabbling in the travel industry will either have to make a serious long-term commitment or disappear. If you think the competition is tough now, just watch how severe it will be in a few years' time.

In fact, we think the next ten years will be the most exciting and progressive in the history of the travel industry. New knowledge, insights, technologies, and methods will complete the conversion of the travel business from a carriage trade operation to a mass-marketed industry.

In most parts of the world, travel and tourism is one of the largest and fastest growing segments of the economy. Ironically, because of its fragmented nature, the travel industry has never been given the recognition it deserves.

As travel becomes more central to the lives of more of the world's population, its contribution to the world economy is better recognized. Consequently, travel is attracting more capital investment and more sophisticated talent.

Marketing will be a key to success in the 1990s. Lip service and slogans will no longer substitute for a real understanding of the marketplace. No longer can we merely respond to market demands. Instead, we must anticipate them by reading Market conditions better and faster than before. The hotel industry is making great strides in this direction. It is moving rapidly from an operations-driven industry to one that is marketing- and consumer-driven. The importance of marketing is apparent, as more CEOs are drawn from the ranks of marketing departments rather than from operations.

If hotel companies are to survive what we call the "no-nonsense 1990s," they must be consumer-driven. Armchair marketing is dead. Instead, companies must gain a better understanding of the wants and needs of their consumers and how best to communicate with them. In so doing, marketers are discovering a sophisticated buyer—one who is well informed and intolerant of slow, boring messages.

The velocity and amount of information that is being disseminated to consumers is growing right along with their ability to consume it. The growth of broadcast media, particularly television, is largely responsible for this acceleration. In industrialized nations, the generations born after World War II have grown tip largely watching TV. Others, without access to TV, have listened to the radio.

As programming and technology improved, viewers and listeners discovered that, compared to print, they are being exposed to more information, more quickly, more vividly, and sometimes more accurately with broadcast media. Generations discovered they could hear about an item faster than they read about it and view a video on it even more quickly.

But television has not replaced newspapers or radio in the marketplace. Instead, people are doing all three—reading, listening, and viewing—thereby consuming far more information. In this process, time has become a precious commodity.

People are generally unwilling to concentrate on slow, complicated, or boring messages. Sometimes even the velocity of televised information is too slow, and people zap through programs, using the remote control on their videocassette recorder. With split screens, viewers can browse more than one program at a time. This behaviour shows conclusively that the mind can comprehend things much faster than we can speak.

As a result, the communicators and advertisers of the future will need to experiment with an efficient new visual and verbal language that can be quickly and easily understood. In print advertising, messages will have to be more simple and similar to billboards, with shorter headlines and more powerful visuals.

Every word and visual must contribute to the message. This impatient consumer has helped drive the technology that speeds the buying decision. Telecommunications, telefaxing, telemarketing, 800 and 900 telephone numbers, and credit-card purchasing are making the traditional coupon-response ads things of the past.

Data-base marketing

As the hotel marketplace becomes more competitive and complex, merely identifying and chasing market segments won't be enough to get the business. We will need to refine these segments further into narrow "slivers," so we can target microsegments. The age of data-base micromarketing is made possible by improved technology. The hotel industry has long been able to capture information about its customers through the registration process. Only in recent years have we seen significant strides in this area. With advanced computer software, hotels will be better able to capture and tabulate customer buying patterns and preferences. With this data base, hotels will be better able to target their marketing and ensure customer satisfaction with the product.

Even as the travel market grows larger, becoming a mass market, hotel companies will have to become more selective about which segments of that market they pursue. Armed with their data base, hotel companies will begin to position themselves against microsegments.

By refining profiles of their customers by using geography, demographics, psychographics, and buying patterns and preferences, hotels will discover nuggets of business opportunities for which they can compete effectively. Moreover, with a deep understanding of their customers, these hotels will be able to tailor their facilities, services, and staff training to their guests' needs. We are convinced that hotel firms large and small that are committed to developing customer data bases will be the ones to compete effectively in the 1990s.

Yield marketing

With the development of data-base marketing, hotel companies will gain a weapon that will benefit revenues, which will constantly be under pressure. Many hotels are already developing yield-management systems that are appropriate to their operations. Yield management can be extended to marketing to create what we have termed "yield marketing." To do this, hotels will need to link their sales, marketing, and reservations systems with their property-management systems. This will be possible because small computers are becoming steadily more flexible and powerful. Yield marketing will link customer responses with the hotel's advertising and promotional efforts. With such a system in place, your hotel will be able accurately and quickly to measure and even anticipate the effectiveness and efficiency of marketing investments. As advertising and sales costs climb, a system like yield marketing will be essential in helping hotels achieve higher returns on advertising and promotion.

Human resources management

During the 1980s, individual hotels and entire hotel chains did whatever they could to differentiate themselves in the consumer's mind. The proliferation of various hotel brands and products was a large factor in this differentiation effort.

In the 1990s, we expect advertising to be an important differentiating factor. The look, quality, style, and tone of properties' advertising will help establish a distinct personality or identity in the marketplace. This personality will also send a signal to employees as to what the hotel stands for.

As facilities and amenities are duplicated from hotel to hotel, consistent staff service and attitude will become substantial differentiating and competitive factors. Hotels that can attract, train, motivate, and hold their employees will have a decided competitive advantage. With the tightening of the labour market, retaining talented employees will be more challenging.

The role of human resources managers will become critical, and all hospitality firms will have to develop innovative recruitment and motivational programs. Hotel managers will have to open two-way communication lines with employees, place more emphasis on a work atmosphere that increases the quality of output, and give greater recognition to the fact that all staff members affect the guest service experience.

First blush

But all these efforts can easily be wasted if a critical factor is overlooked—namely, the person who closes the sale. The hotel industry spends hundreds of millions of dollars to develop beautiful and elaborate advertising campaigns to get potential customers to do one thing. That thing is to dial the number of the hotel's reservation desk or system. And who does that customer talk to when he or she calls for a reservation? Almost always, the least seasoned, perhaps lowest paid member of our sales staff answers the call.

In most cases, the reservationist is the first employee to talk to the customer. Shouldn't this person be the most motivated and best informed member of our staff ? If not, all the merchandising efforts in the world will not close the sale. Companies like Disney are leading the way in employee training, so that every staff member is immersed in company culture and ready to serve the guest in an appropriate fashion.

Bonding

Once the new customer has been won, hotels face the challenge of keeping that customer. It costs hotel companies five to six times as much to win new customers as to keep them. But today's notoriously fickle customer has little brand loyalty. To promote more loyalty, hotel operators are beginning to realize they must stay close to their customers, listen to them, and satisfy their wants and needs.

By personalizing the guest experience, we can build the customer's loyalty and create repeat business. Advertising, too, must become more important and relevant. As advertising plays an increasing role in winning new customers and keeping the old, the credibility of the message will determine its underlying effectiveness. We must place our message and our hotel name in the context of our customers' lives. The closer we can relate the hotel to our prospect's lifestyle, the closer that person will feel to the hotel, the more effective the advertising message will be, and the stronger the brand loyalty. Burleigh Gardner calls this "bonding," and we see evidence of it in a greater number of consumer advertising messages.

Hotel advertising seems to be lagging behind consumer products in attempting in getting consumers to bond to the hotel brand. That job will fall not just on advertising campaigns but on all levels of hotel employees. These are the challenges of the 1990s: Give the consumer your message and be quick about it. Deliver on your promises in such a way that the consumer is aware of an open, two-way communication with your establishment, Bring employees into the picture by understanding their needs. Pay attention to micromarketing and explore the possibilities of yield marketing.

Selling to group markets

Selling to group markets in the hotel business is both an art as well as a science. The science side deals with applying the principles of marketing and management to hospitality selling. Product positioning, market segmentation, target marketing, and sales management are all practiced in hospitality group market sales, just as they are selling strategies in any industry. The "art" reflects the reality of intuition, common sense, good judgment, and decency in dealing with customers, clients, owners, employees, and the community-at-large. In other words, management theory usually works but must always be weighed by good instincts and "using your head."

Clients and customers

Selling hotel space means considering the needs of both clients and customers. Clients are the persons responsible for planning the event—be it a company's annual sales conference, a group holiday tour, a national medical association convention, or a family reunion. Customers are the people who actually attend the event. These include the conference attendees, the association convention delegates, the individuals who purchased the holiday tour package, or the family members attending the family reunion.

Hotel sales managers deal primarily with clients. It is their job to find out the needs of the potential clients and their respective customers, and then to determine whether the hotel can fulfil those needs. These needs typically include the hotel guest rooms, meeting rooms, banquet facilities, hospitality suites, and so forth.

Location of the hotel, access to airports and highways, recreation facilities, and service amenities are also common criteria that clients consider when booking with a hotel. Once the meeting is "booked," it is the job of the entire hotel management team to ensure that the needs of the client and their respective customers are, indeed, met.

Group markets

The needs of a meeting planner, an event coordinator, a tour broker, or a football coach travelling with his team do vary. Thus, the group market is segmented by various types of groups that share common needs. In turn, most hotel marketers identify one or more of these group market segments as their specific target market(s) for their respective hotels. This not only helps the hotel to be better positioned in the marketplace, it also gives the hotel sales staff focus in its selling efforts to identified target market needs.

Market segments for hotel sales may include associations and conventions, corporations, government, education, sports, medical, incentive travel, and group tours. Though not an exhaustive list, each group represents a major market in hotel convention sales. Following is a brief description of each.

Association and convention market

Of the major group markets, associations and conventions are probably the most widely written about, read about, and known about. They range from small regional associations such as the New England Rose Growers Association to meganational associations such as the 12,000-member American Bankers Association. Associations meet regularly, most often on an annual basis. Throughout North America these meetings are commonly known as the "annual convention." The association and convention market can be further segmented by the type of organization. These include trade associations, professional associations, and the "SMERF" association grouping, which includes social, military, educational, religious, and fraternal organizations. Because of the largely nonprofit nature of SMERF organizations, they tend to be more price-sensitive than the trade and professional associations.

Corporate market

Corporations of all sizes hold various off-premise meetings, conferences, and conventions. Typical locations for these meetings are hotels, resorts, and conference centers. The various types of corporate meetings include sales and marketing, training, management, professional/technical, and stockholder. They can range in size from 10 to 1,000+ attendees meeting annually, semiannually, or quarterly. Some larger corporations have professional meeting planning departments that plan all the company's meetings, whereas others leave the job of meeting planning to the department head or division head who is calling the meeting.

Government market

Many hotels specifically target the government market largely because of its sheer size. For example, almost 15 percent of the U.S. workforce is employed by local, state, and federal government agencies. Most government off-premise meetings are educational seminars and/or training programs. Government meeting planning is quite different from that of the private sector; special attention needs to be paid to specific government regulations and restrictions, per diems, and special budget and billing procedures. The Society of Government Meeting Planners addresses the specific needs of meeting planning for all levels of government.

Education market

The education market for hotel convention sales is an often misunderstood market, most likely because it is quite broad and has component parts in other major markets. The education market includes secondary and higher education institutions such as private schools and public universities, education associations such as the National Association of English Teachers, and corporate education and training seminars.

The main reason for the education market's potential as a selected target market is its breadth, its repeat business potential, and its willingness to meet during traditionally slow periods. First, the education market is broad in scope and cuts across many industry sectors, including profit and nonprofit organizations. Second, the repeat business potential is strong, especially from large institutions with a multitude of divisions and activities. Targeting a university, for example, would include soliciting business from the academic units, the alumni office, the division of continuing education, and so forth. Third, and perhaps most important, many education-oriented conferences meet during the summer months, which is typically a slow period for corporate, trade, and professional association convention activity. As noted earlier, the education market is price-sensitive as well. Thus, "matching" the price needs of this market will help fill empty guest rooms during an off-peak summer period.

Sports market

Professional and collegiate team sports constitute the major portion of the sports market. Professional individual sporting events such as golf and tennis and amateur sporting events such as figure skating championships are also part of this growing market. A key aspect for soliciting the sports market is understanding the specific needs of the coach and/or sponsor of the event.

Typical requests include close proximity to where the sporting event is taking place, special menus and meal times, unusual checkin and checkout times, extra security and privacy, large guest rooms, and special billing procedures.

Medical market

The medical market is comprised of health care professionals in medicine and related disciplines attending seminars, symposiums, and workshops for their particular field. Sponsors of these conferences include universities, private institutions, medical associations, clinics, and the like. Research and technology, in particular, have spurred tremendous growth in the medical meetings group market where there is a pressing need to keep pace with the latest advancements in the medical profession.

Particular needs of the medical market for hotel marketers to consider include a short booking lead time, high-tech audio-visual equipment, and guest rooms accommodating work/ study space, for instance, large desks, good lighting, and quiet.

Medical meetings meet often and regularly, and their meeting planners are very meticulous in their demands. Though sometimes considered difficult to deal with, they usually respond quite favourably to a professional approach in assisting with their meeting needs.

Incentive travel market

Incentive travel is a reward to salespeople, dealers, distributors, and employees by management. It offers travel for goals and/or achievements reached over a specified period of time. Incentive travel is largely a motivational tool and management often hires professionally managed incentive travel companies to develop and implement their programs.

The incentive planner is looking to develop a program that will provide a memorable experience for the participants. Thus, criteria such as an exciting destination, variety of entertainment options, creativity in food and beverage functions, and recreation alternatives are important for the hotel and site selection decision. The incentive travel market is a lucrative one and hotels offering attractive destinations actively seek this business.

Group tour market

The group tour market is huge and complex. In this market one can be dealing with a number of players, including wholesalers, retailers, tour brokers, and travel clubs. Because of its complexity, most hotels that target this market usually have one or more sales managers who specialize in it. In essence, the group tour market meets the needs of individuals who wish to travel for pleasure with other groups of people. Instead of setting their own itinerary, they seek the help of a professional travel planner who assists with the selection of an itinerary. The itinerary may be a prepackaged tour offered by a tour wholesaler, a travel club developing its own itinerary, or simply a charter to reach a predetermined destination at a discounted price.

The sales process

Target marketing is essential for successful selling to group markets in the hospitality industry. Once target markets have been identified it is important to understand the basic tenets of the sales process. The five major steps of the sales process are given below:

1. *Open the Relationship*: Current accounts, prospecting, leads and referrals.
2. *Qualify the Account*: Determine needs and wants both tangible and intangible in past and present.
3. *Present the Message*: Provide "solutions" to "problems" through features and benefits offered by the hotel.
4. *Close the Sale*: Ask for the business and "book" the account.
5. *Service the Account*: Deliver as promised.

Open the relationship

The obvious first step is to open a relationship with a potential client. There are numerous sources and the best place to start is with current accounts. Trace dates or tickler files are commonly used by sales managers as a reminder to periodically check with regular accounts about upcoming meetings, events, or newly planned conferences. Other sources include prospecting, leads, and referrals. Prospecting is calling on potential clients who have not met previously at the hotel but have the potential to do so. For example, if a new division of AT&T recently relocated in an area, a sales manager from the hotel should make a sales call to learn about their off-premise meeting activity, who plans the meetings, and where the meetings typically take place. Prospecting is often times initially done by phone and then followed up with a personal sales call to identified potential clients. Leads and referral are opportunities for potential business from an outside source.

Qualify the account

Qualifying a potential account is twofold. The current needs and wants of the meeting planner must be identified. This includes both the physical as well as the psychological needs of the meeting being planned. The physical needs refer to the largely tangible aspects of the event such as number of persons attending, duration of the conference, number of guest rooms required, number and size of meetings and banquets to be scheduled, and so on.

Present the message

Once the needs and wants, both tangible and intangible, have been identified, the sales manager is now in a position to present the message. This is usually done in person at the hotel and then followed up with a letter of proposal or letter of agreement.

This letter of agreement includes all pertinent items discussed during the negotiations such as dates, rates, number of guest rooms to be reserved, major food functions, and credit policy. Once both parties have signed the letter of agreement it then becomes a contract. A key point in presenting the message is that the sales manager provide "solutions" for the meeting planner's "problems.". The tenet of marketing is that you—the supplier—can provide the consumer with what he or she needs. In hotel sales it is the facilities and services of a lodging establishment that are provided to house, feed, and entertain the attendees of a meeting, conference, or convention. The meeting planner sets the objective(s) for the meeting, not the management of the hotel. However, it is the job of the hotelier to ensure the meeting planner be given the facilities and services to help meet those objectives.

"Book it" is hospitality sales vernacular for closing the sale. It means that a signed contract from the meeting planner has been received by the hotel and that reservations for the guest rooms, meeting rooms, and banquet functions are "on the books." The event may be scheduled for two months away or ten years out. And it may have taken anywhere from two weeks to two years or more to open the relationship, qualify the account, present the message, and close the sale. Nonetheless, it is now booked and preparation for servicing the account begins. Servicing the account may or may not be the job responsibility of the hotel sales manager. In larger hotels, the account is often turned over to the convention services department. However, the sales manager continues to keep in touch with the client even if he or she now shares joint responsibility with a convention services manager assigned to the account.

Service the account

Servicing the account entails collecting all the many details that need to be pulled together prior to the event taking place. These include such items as specific meeting room setups, audio-visual requirements, VIP lists, suite accommodations, food function menus, rooming lists, billing instructions, credit arrangements, storage of shipments to the hotel, ground transportation requests, schedule changes, and so forth.

A few weeks prior to arrival a convention resume is developed outlining the specific details for the group. It is an internal document disseminated to all department heads in the hotel. For larger groups and/or complex events a preconvention meeting is often held. Here, the meeting planner confers with key department heads to review the convention resume, clarify any questions that arise, and go over the inevitable last minute changes.

Either the sales manager is responsible for delivery or it is assigned to a convention services manager. Whichever, there should always be some member of management assigned to each account to follow through and be available during the entire event. Recent studies have shown that having one staff member be responsible for and responsive to the meeting planner during the event adds substantially to overall client satisfaction with the hotel and its services.

Client—finding

Marketing is all about getting and keeping a client. Sales is charged with getting a client—finding out who needs what and where the "fit" fits. Hotel operations is charged with keeping a client by delivering a product or service that meets and exceeds customer expectations. In other words, we want more than just a satisfied customer, we want the customer to return again, again, and again.

Relationship marketing

Relationship marketing is very much involved with getting and keeping a customer. It views a sale as part of a process, not as an isolated goal to be obtained. In relationship marketing the customer is viewed as an asset of the firm. As an asset, the customer becomes as important to management as does the building, the equipment, the inventory, and the employee.

Strategic analysis

The primary purpose of strategic analysis is to give planners a platform from which to review the significance of their firm's market situation and to think about options in dealing with it. Strategic analysis consists of the SWOT analysis (strengths, weaknesses, opportunities, and threats) and the strategic analysis questioning sequence.

The SWOT analysis is the detailed search and listing of factors from the situational analysis that might or will impact the business's strategy Strategic marketing is based on the SWOT analysis. The process by which SWOT factors are derived is to carefully review the internal analysis for strengths and weaknesses, and the environmental analysis for opportunities and threats, and to then record, in the appropriate category, every factor that has a reasonable possibility of affecting the short- and long-term future of the firm.

From a marketing standpoint, the primary purpose of the SWOT analysis is to serve as a framework to guide the selection of key opportunities in the environment. These opportunities will subsequently be matched up with appropriate strengths of the business.

The secondary purpose is to identify and analyze potential or actual threats that could hurt the business, and weaknesses in key areas that may need to be upgraded to allow the business to compete more successfully. Collectively, weaknesses and threats are often referred to as "problems." On paper, most weaknesses can be corrected; but in the real world, a business may have to live with some imperfections or less than exemplary skills or assets.

The selection of opportunities to pursue, threats to defend against, and weaknesses to correct is not a simple matter. The company's abilities and trends in the marketplace, particularly customer demands and competitors' strategies, are always changing. The purpose of the SWOT analysis is to offer a menu from which one can objectively view the possible alternatives, not to make the selection automatic.

Strategic analysis questioning sequence

Developing strategies is not a great challenge. Most firms prepare annual marketing plans that contain reasonably well-thought-out strategies that will keep the firm at or near its present competitive position. But the challenge and the ultimate responsibility of market managers are not to keep firms in their current position. To survive in a dynamic environment, businesses must grow in strength by finding strategies that allow it to stand out from competitors. Finding the right strategy does not guarantee success.

Need for models

Once management has decided that it is worth its effort to search for viable alternative strategies and attempt to settle on probable strategic directions for the firm, a major question surfaces. "How do I distinguish between what is important and what is not?" Before this question is answered it is important to understand four issues. First, no human on earth can know everything about a situation as complicated as a firm's competitive environment. Even if he/she did, too many things can change, making the initial prediction at least partially obsolete. The objective is not to know everything, but to know and understand what is important and relevant to the issues being addressed. Second, a million dollar research program can help explain and predict certain phenomena. However, no amount of research will ever be complete enough to encompass all potential issues. Third, corporate culture and politics will often have a greater influence on decisions than the facts on which the decisions are based. And fourth, managers with different mental models will describe the same situation differently.

The crucible of strategic decisions

In the planning process, management develops extensive lists of SWOT factors. These various situational factors are then analyzed to decide which are important enough to act on, which should be monitored and considered for the future, and which should be given tertiary status. While most firms view the strategic analysis process as important, few give it the attention it deserves. Since selected strategies are the foundation for the success or failure of the company, strategic analysis is the crucible of the decision-making process.

Strategic decision-making

Whether explicit or implicit, all firms have some type of plan for the future. The quality of these plans is often correlated with the quality of information and processes or models used to develop them. If management has historically developed successful strategies, then these efforts should probably be continued, regardless of their foundation in managerial science and theory.

When management has had difficulty in producing effective strategies, or strategic options are not forthcoming, a formal means of analysis-a model-should be considered. Too often when the word strategy is used an aura of permanence is assumed. Thirty or forty years ago this may have been true. Today, change comes quickly What appeared logical a few months ago may appear half-baked today Strategy is the first step or starting point of business decision-making. It is initially conceived as a business strategy that will be supported by functional strategies and tactics.

The theoretical foundation for all decisions

Regardless of the decision style employed, all decisions involve the concepts of strategic issues diagnosis and vigilant information processing.

Strategic issues diagnois (SID)

This analytical concept refers to the degree of effort utilized when diagnosing or examining an issue. Strategic issues diagnosis is divided into two categories, active (reflective) and automatic (unreflective) SID. Active SID is a systematic means of reviewing information for decision-making, especially for critical issues. Because of the issues' importance, management must utilize a process or model to assure that critical information is on hand and that alternative solutions are thoroughly examined. Active SID is also known as procedural rationality. Rationality is this instance is defined as the extent to which information is collected for a decision and the degree of reliance on analysis of the information to make a decision.

The alternative to the active SID (or procedural rationality) decision-making processes is termed automatic SID. This occurs when the decision-maker's experience with the issue induces an automatic diagnosis-intuition. There are both problems and advantages with automatic SID. The primary problems are that one's experience may produce outdated means of addressing the issue, and that new, perhaps more suitable, means are ignored or are given only cursory attention. Another problem with automatic SID occurs during the annual planning process or during crises. In these circumstances decisions are being made that will impact the long-term future of the business; they should therefore be given reasonable consideration before strategies are selected. There are advantages to automatic SID, but caution must be used. The primary advantage is that it preserves executives' valuable time and capacity for attention to a variety of decisions by letting them utilize their experience and judgment.

Vgilant information processing (VIP)

Herb Simon developed a model of decision-making similar to the active/ automatic SID typology. He said that decisions (planning decisions, in this case) are made under low, medium, or high stress. Decisions made under low stress tend to result in either doing nothing, utilizing the existing strategy, or acting without searching for more viable alternatives. Though the vast majority of hotels and restaurants do not operate in low-stress environments, they tend to make marketing decisions as if they were. This is evidenced by the fact that too many of these firms simply dust off last year's marketing plan and reuse it.

Moderate-stress decisions have the best chance for a thorough search and appraisal or vigilant information processing. This is the optimal level of stress for decision-making. Marketers know that the decision is very important, but since they are in control of the situation, they can summon all their abilities to make the necessary decision(s). The steps for vigilant information processing include (1) setting an objective that, if met, will satisfy specific and overall organizational goals; (2) searching for strategies and tactics that will achieve the objective; and then, (3) when a strategy (or tactic) is found that would likely achieve the objective, the search is stopped and the strategy is incorporated into the organization's plan. One of Simon's theories was that a business can rarely optimize its strategy search.

Optimizing meant that marketers would search for all possible alternative strategies or tactics. Marketers must instead suboptimize, or find the best alternative after a reasonable search. The two primary threats to VIP are procrastination (putting off the decision) or buck-passing (letting someone else make the decision). Decisions made under high stress are generally not effective because the decision-maker cannot function at his/her optimal capacity.

Strategic analysis questions

The key tasks of the marketing information system were earlier described as deciding which data are necessary, then gathering, storing, and analyzing the data for decision-making purposes. Decisions on necessary data gathering and storing of data are relatively simple tasks. As long as an organized process is in place, most activities prior to analysis (formal research being the main exception) can be accomplished by personnel with limited research experience.

Basically, management must make sure that a sufficient database has been compiled that will help decision-makers see the big picture. Effective analysis, and the subsequent diagnosis and decisions that follow, will require a much higher level of cognitive skills. Sitting around a table with a few environmental reports and internal records will not likely produce the most favorable results. A problem with the all-too-common cursory analysis is that five people will come up with five different solutions to the same situation. Unfortunately, since their opinions may be subjective and based on conjecture rather than analysis, each solution will be defended personally, producing dissension rather than consensus. The most skillful debater and those with political power will be heard above those with worthy and substantive concepts, perspectives, and strategic options.

While most firms view the analysis and diagnosis

process as important, few give it the attention it deserves. Since it leads to decisions on future objectives and strategies, and therefore the potential success or failure of the company, the analysis of SWOT factors is actually the crucible of decision-makers and the planning process. This is the primary area where inferential skills come into play. To improve the likelihood of consensus and to reduce the inherent risk involved in business decisions, some type of organized review or process of analysis should be considered.

The primary purpose of analysis at this point in the planning process is not to finalize the firm's strategies: it is to make sure that decision-makers have a detailed knowledge and understanding of the firm's competitive position and available strategic choices and to develop a consensus on the general direction in which many of its most important strategies should be headed. This analysis aids in the setting of longterm and annual objectives; corporate, business, and functional strategies; and related policies and action plans.

For example, a preliminary assessment of a firm's opportunities for growth and related optional strategies will lead to a more realistic setting of objectives and better strategy selection. It also provides a platform for brainstorming of "alternative" strategies that may not have been considered in a formal discussion and forces the company to review its existing strategies for soundness in light of new environmental data and the changing abilities of the firm

Strategic analysis of SWOT factors [a form of active strategic issues diagnosis (SID)] entails asking a series of ten questions to elicit and guide management's opinion of the relevance and value of a particular factor or group of factors and the firm's potential strategic direction. Though the process might at first appear somewhat laborious, it can actually be accomplished very quickly. The choice is basically between an organized process that guides the business in thoroughly analyzing key factors, and random subjective opinions that lead to strategies with minimal factual support.

The number of SWOT factors that should be strategically analyzed depends on their perceived importance to the success of the business. In the actual planning process, only the most significant SWOT factors or groups of factors will be formally analyzed. Since many firms will group related SWOT factors, such as those concerned with increasing banquet business, the process may need to be reviewed only a few times. It can be completed via written reports or oral review.

As the questioning process is ingrained in the subconscious thought processes of management and marketing decision-makers, most SWOT factors can quickly be reviewed for their implications, importance, an possible solutions or strategies. Some actors can be processed in a few minutes. Others will take several days or longer if critical information is required for a thorough analysis. Occasionally, an item is weeded out after one or two of the questions, if it is felt that further discussion for that SWOT factor is not necessary.

Market position

1. What is the firm's current market position?

Before a firm can attempt to capitalize on opportunities from its particular competitive situation, it must first have a reasonable idea of how it is viewed by its current target customers (its objective position). The categories include the following: position #1, a leader in the market; position #2, somewhat ahead of the market; position #3, meeting current market demand; position #4, slightly behind market demand; position #5, seriously behind market demand. With its current position in mind, the marketers can then decide on the degree of strategy change appropriate for its particular competitive position.

SWOT fcator analysis

2. What are the key SWOT factors that must be evaluated in the plan?

The business must now select those factors from the SWOT analysis that have the greatest possibility for impacting the firm in a positive or negative manner. Since the SWOT analysis is a summary of the situation analysis, this question is essentially asking, "What information do we have that is important enough to require action?" For example, in a firm's SWOT analysis, there could be 100 or more potential opportunities listed. It would not be economically or logistically feasible to try to take advantage of each, so only those with the greatest potential to further the firm's competitive position will be selected. Since the primary objective of the marketing department is to increase sales, opportunities with the potential to increase sales are generally considered first. Subsequently, the firm should address threats that must be defended against, weaknesses that must be corrected, and whether strengths are being fully maximized.

Grouping factors

When possible, related issues should be grouped together into a smaller number of major issues. This combining of factors allows the firm to effectively broaden the number of issues that will become part of its analysis and possibly its strategy. For example, weaknesses in the areas of per person revenue, front-desk courtesy, cleanliness, and food waste might be attributed to the larger problem of a lack of or ineffective training, no training manuals, weak management, and so on. The fact that people want more security in hotels and are taking shorter trips, that the American's with Disabilities Act mandates accommodations for most disabilities; that there are more older people traveling; that older people are quite value-conscious and want health-oriented meals and enjoy continental breakfasts, could be combined to go after the senior citizen market.

Judging the important SWOT factors

Some means such as prioritization, impact/ immediacy analysis, or confidence assessment should be utilized to assess the importance of the various factors in the firm's situational analysis.

Prioritisation: If SWOT factors, or groups of related SWOT factors, are prioritized by degree of importance, it will allow management to focus its efforts in areas that will produce the best results. Prioritization could be indicated by listing and numbering according to degree of importance, or by assigning levels of importance such as A = high priority, B = secondary or medium priority and C = low priority. An entirely new marketing department for a competing hotel made up of experienced veterans might be labeled "A," a new director of sales or the creation of an instate sales manager's position for this competing hotel might be given a "B" rating, and the hiring of a new sales manager might be labeled "C" or possibly ignored if the skill level of the new sales manager was approximately the same as the former sales manager.

Impact and immediacy: A means of determining the importance of a threat or opportunity as well as a strength or a weakness is to assess its potential:

— impact-how great an effect it could have

— immediacy-the likelihood of it occurring, how soon it might take place, and if it did occur, how long the firm would have to prepare a strategy or tactic for it

If the determination is that it would have very little impact and no potential effect for several years, then it may not be necessary to include it in the analysis. If, on the other hand, the determination was positive, then it should probably be included in the analysis. In essence, this helps marketers and management differentiate between burnt toast and tragedy.

Two factors may be serious, but one may have the potential for great harm, while another is simply a nuisance. For example, if a budget hotel had an excellent location in an area with several hotel sites, the company would have to consider the immediacy of a competitor constructing a hotel on the site and the impact it would have. If the determination of immediacy could be expressed as "potentially within a year," and its impact could be significant, then an applicable strategy would be implemented, or at least a contingency plan would be written and available if needed.

Confidence: The revelance of data or information can be assigned to categories based on the level of confidence attached to its probability of occurring. The categories could be identified by various titles. Most commonly used are high, medium, and low confidence data. This labeling could assist and alert marketers so that when a factor is discussed, decision-makers within the firm would understand how likely the event is to happen or how much weight the firm gives to its occurring. For example, the likelihood of increased demands for nutritious foods could be considered as high-confidence information, while the measurement of the availability of Alaskan salmon and the assessment of its market price might be low-confidence information.

3. What are the implications of the key SWOT factor or groups of factors being considered?

Of the key SWOT factors listed, the firm must determine

their relevance for further analysis. This question is central to the analysis and extrapolation of information from the selected key SWOT factors. It is essentially asking the question, "How does or could this factor (or group of factors) affect the firm, its customers, or competitors?"

One of the abilities required to develop potential implications of a SWOT factor is a manager's inferential skill-the ability to identify relevant issues and recognize the degree of their importance. Essentially, this means being able to analyze information and form valid assumptions that will assist in decision-making.

For example, a high level of guest satisfaction (a strength) may imply that there is an opportunity for sales growth through both existing units and expansion. Lower sales than desired (a weakness) could have many implications: for example, the firm's product or service mix is not what customers want; the firm has been promoting an inferior product or service; the firm has not promoted its offering effectively (assuming a quality product or service); or the firm is not in a position to expand at the present time.

If customers want more seafood (an opportunity), this would imply that additional seafood items should be considered, possibly an image change or repositioning is needed, and area competitors' seafood offerings should carefully be examined along with competitors that may also be considering adding seafood. If there is a possible price or value war (a threat), the implication could be that value should be a primary concern in the pricing and production of all menu items; that to remain competitive, costs should be minimized to the greatest extent possible; and that some or all menu items should be positioned as good or great values.

Intution: Knowing something without conscious reasoning plays a part in the analysis of implications. The part of the mind used for this level of thought is the subconscious. Basically, this is where all previously acquired knowledge-the sum of a person's experiences-is stored.

Developing implications requires a deep thought process that generally accelerates based on the degree of experience and ability of an individual to bring that experience to bear on the analysis. Where brainstorming, also an excellent method of eliciting ideas, brings an active, vocal participation from group members, intuition is best utilized in a quiet, relaxed atmosphere (better individually than in a group) allowing people to bring up their deepest thoughts.

Frequently, the most in-depth understanding of a situation comes within about 30 minutes after lying down, when an individual is almost asleep, or the following day, by remembering dreams. The reason why relaxation, meditation, or sleep increases mental ability is because the mind is most effective when the brainwave cycles are at lower levels. There is much validity to the adage, "I'll sleep on it." Intuition can also be used to help develop optional strategies or the solutions to other problems or situations.

Historical experience with key SWOT factors

4. Have existing strategies related to key SWOT factors been effective?

Essentially, every existing strategy the firm now has was directly or indirectly based on a particular past SWOT factor. If a particular strategy has been successful, and its related SWOT factors have not changed, the company should consider keeping it as long as it is compatible with the new environment. If related environmental factors have changed, then the strategy will need to be reassessed and perhaps discontinued, markedly changed, or at least modified.

In cases where the strategy has not been successful, it should either be dropped or reconsidered based on the new SWOT analysis. If the cause of the problem is with execution and not a misreading of the competitive market, it must be addressed as a weakness. In this instance, a determination should be made as to whether the weakness is possible to correct or its cost in resources, including time, are worth the effort.

For example, a hypothetical restaurant is analyzing the SWOT factor of customers wanting a place to eat after 2 a.m. when the bars close down. In the past, the firm had tried to take advantage of the opportunity, but it was not successful. The firm would have to consider whether there have been changes in its strengths and weaknesses that might allow it to be more successful this time.

Additionally, are there any changes in the impact or immediacy of the opportunities? Is there a larger market for late-night food service now than in the past, or is the market more willing to frequent a restaurant offering late-night service? Perhaps there are more restaurants or clubs in the vicinity that are helping to increase the size of the market and their inclination to visit the area.

Overall, everything the company now does should be put on trial for its life. The only sacred cow for a business should be its morals and philosophy of doing business. Strategies, like consumer behavior, must be flexible. Unfortunately, there is a tendency for firms to continue existing strategies whether they were successful or not.

Executives who have decided to pursue a certain

course that has not been successful will often not want to change positions because it is tantamount to admitting failure. Naturally, this unwillingness to change will almost invariably lead to the executive's replacement. The primary reasons for this are that:

— Millions of dollars may have been lost and stockholders want a change.

— A new executive with appropriate skills may be needed to help select and implement new strategies.

— The executive is unable or unwilling to change.

Hospitality trade magazines frequently detail stories about changes in the executive suite. Because of stockholder distrust and increased publicity regarding high pay for poor performance, it is expected that these changes will not only continue but are likely to surge.

Future alternative strategies

5. What alternative or optional strategies should be considered?

The alternative strategies will be developed from a screening of the SWOT analysis for potentially profitable opportunities, strengths that should be maximized, weaknesses that must be corrected, and threats that should be avoided or defended against. For example, if a new market segment has been identified that could increase sales—an opportunity—then alternative strategies to take advantage of it would be developed.

Alternative strategies must be based, as much as possible, on an objective appraisal of the firm's situational analysis. Marketing planners' experience or personal feelings about the environmental concern or optional strategies often lead to an automatic diagnosis. In some cases, this may be the most effective and efficient means to the strategy decision.

After all, most decisions (strategies and tactics) are the result of personal experience and the success of past decisions. To determine their viability the alternative strategies (also referred to as strategic options) would then be subjected to strategic issue diagnosis, through the remaining strategic analysis questions.

If a firm has certain exceptional strengths, especially sustainable competitive advantages, with which to take advantage of the SWOT factor, it can develop strategies to extract the greatest value from the strength. For example, if a hotel's strength was having a location near every major airport in the United States, then alternative strategies based on this could be developed. The firm would take advantage of the opportunity of potential business from airline customers and employees based on the strength of its locations.

The marketing department could develop a promotional strategy around that fact, such as offering a special rate to all major firms that fly into those airports, offering a special rate to airline crews and placing signs in the airport stressing the convenient location.

When a firm's strengths are not considered formidable, the goal might be to direct the company's efforts at developing strategies designed to fill a niche in the market not currently being addressed. An independent restaurant operator could focus on personal service, high-quality menu offerings, specials, serving regional favorites, and other strategies that might differentiate it from chain operators.

Similarly, when a firm considers weaknesses it must develop alternative strategies to correct them. When a skill that is needed to take advantage of an attractive opportunity does not exist—a weakness—management must decide whether it is worth the effort to make appropriate changes-implement a strategy to correct it.

Defending against threats (defensive strategies) poses a more difficult problem. If the actions of a competitor, societal trends, changes in traveling habits, or trends in any other area of the environment indicate a possible or probable threat, management must decide if it is necessary to prepare a strategy to defend against the threat. Often, other actions of the firm are normally already helping to defend against the threat.

For example, if a threat is posed by a primary competitor's high RPPQ (relative perceived product/ service quality), or if such a competitor is planning on moving into an existing firm's trade area, the existing firm would probably already have a strategy in place to upgrade its products and services.

Under normal circumstances, this practice should be a never-ending strategy. Additional defenses, such as price, quantity, or plate appearance adjustments, might also be considered. The key question here would be, "What do I need to do. (what strategy or tactic is needed) to successfully defend the firm against the perceived threat?"

Not acting on some SWOT factors is unavoidable. The company can only do so much. But an increasingly common characteristic of business strategies is the inaction on imminent and serious threats. Unfortunately, too many firms, especially smaller businesses, view themselves as being unable to mount a defense against a larger competitor.

In almost all cases of fair competition, there are strategies by which even the smallest competitor can protect itself and even thrive in the midst of large competitors. In fact, smaller and leaner competitors often have major strengths that can be exploited, such as the ability to adapt quicker to changing market conditions, more personalized service, and lower overhead.

A decision must be made as to which factors should be acted on immediately, spread out over the short- or longterm future, or put off indefinitely. Someone must lead the firm and take responsibility for deciding which path to take.

Locating optional strategies

The search for strategies is analytical, creative, incremental, and political.

Analytical: Marketing has been perceived as a discipline where creative thought was the predominant requirement. This attitude does not do justice to the study. Creativity is important, but it makes up only a small portion of the marketer's requisite skills. The primary reason people perceive marketing as a creative activity is because most firms lack a formal plan to guide the decision process.

It is true that marketing does require some creativity but the critical academic requirement for hospitality marketing is actually analytical. The marketer first does research to establish various facts about the firm and its environment.

Marketing creativity flows directly from the quality and quantity of that research. From this information, marketing managers decide what products or services the customer will purchase, other marketing mix variables such as pricing and atmosphere, and, finally, how to communicate these to potential consumers.

Creative. Everyone is creative to a degree: but the difference between average creativity and superior creativity is the difference between an occasional jogger and an Olympic athlete. The first step to creativity in a business organization is to have an environment conducive to creativity. The following are some of the characteristics of a "creative organization":

Receptive to new ideas, sensitive to different possible approaches, withholding judgment or criticism

Attitude of the organization as a whole

Attitude of each individual's supervisor

Recognition

Time for creative thought, away from normal responsibilities

Freedom of choice to do what is reasonably necessary to pursue one's ideas

The physical environment of the workplace

The amount of interaction between workers

For marketing, the process of developing a new product or service includes idea generation (seeking a reasonable quantity of new ideas that appear to solve the issue at hand), idea screening (deciding which ideas have the most potential), and concept development (creating and testing the ideas).

Creative idea generation begins by getting into the minds of customers. What do they want? How do they think? What are their behaviors relative to the firm's products and services? When the average firm attempts to use creative thinking it will normally use convergent thinking-focusing on the one best solution.

One of the keys to maximizing the creative process is the use of divergent thinking-not setting parameters on ideas and attempting to gather the largest quantity of options rather than the best quality options. Qualitative concerns would be addressed later if an option was considered for adoption. Some basic forms of creative thinking are the following:

— *Attribute listing.* Simply list the various attributes for which the customer is looking-ideally, those that delve into the psychology and motivational characteristics of potential customers.

— *Forced relationships.* Select any stimulus word, list the characteristics of that word, and then determine which of those words have any possible relationship or application to the firm's strategies or procedures. For example, the stimulus word is "canned tomatoes." Its characteristics and uses are: red, watery, salty acid, bright, mushy, crushed, seeds, silver, metal, paper, Italian, spaghetti sauce, tomato soup, and so forth. These characteristics would then be viewed as to how they could be applied to any desired strategy or procedure. This could range from another food item to the decor of a restaurant.

- *Fantasy technique.* This method is utilized by an individual in private. The person sits in a comfortable chair in a quiet room. The task is to visualize oneself as a customer going through the hotel or restaurant, while sensing all the smells, sounds, decor/ atmosphere, furniture/ fixtures, and people one would encounter. Immediately afterward, all thoughts, feelings, and ideas are recorded. The insights are used to develop possible improvements, modifications, and innovations.

— *Heuristic Ideation Technique (HIT).* (Heuristic refers to a self-guided method of developing solutions to a problem.) This is the utilization of a matrix to establish possible relationships. On the vertical side of the matrix could be the entrees that will be served in the restaurant. On the horizontal side could be the various styles of serving pieces that are available. Then, each block or grid in the matrix would be considered for its possibilities. The selection of plates, entrees, and the analysis could be more extensive. The HIT grid is commonly used to develop new menu items. The available meats, poultry, and seafood items would be placed on one side of the matrix, and the possible accompaniments on the other. For example, a chicken breast could be paired with mushrooms, green onion, garlic, basil, wine, tomatoes, and mozzarella cheese. The objective in this case is not only promotion of creativity but also cross-utilization of existing products.

	Ingredients		
Salads	Red Bell Peppers	Artichoke Hearts	Mushrooms
Chef Salad	Yes	Maybe	Yes
Tuna Salad	Yes	No	No
Chicken Fajita	Yes	No	No
Salmon Chef	Yes	Yes	Yes
Dinner Salad	No	No	No

Figure 1: Heuristic ideation technique

— *Collective notebook method.* This is simply a small notebook that is carried at all times. When a thought comes up, write it down. It is especially useful if placed by the bed, because as the mind relaxes, its capacity for creativity increases. Analyze the material for possible application.

Conventional wisdom should be discarded when developing potential strategies. Often, unconventional strategies or tactics that initially sound far-fetched bring up other ideas with potential for implementation. A television commercial showing pizza with cheese that stretches throughout the house is definitely not mainstream, but it worked. The target customer desired humor. These "illogical" strategies may also offer a window to the future needs of the customer-the potential to reach position 1. Since strategies are developed for the short and long term, the longer the lead time the stranger the potential strategy will sound. Operational and financial creativity are concerned primarily with effectiveness and efficiency. How can we do something better, faster, or at a lower cost? It is important not to have preconceptions of how things should be done.

Incremental. The search is incremental because the selection process begins by analyzing past strategies, policies, and marketing action plans to decide what has been successful and what has not. Actions that have been successful are kept, those that are not are discontinued or modified, and new strategies are "incrementally" added to existing strategies, policies, or action plans. For example, if a functional strategy to control costs has been successful in reducing costs by the amount set in the annual objectives, then the strategy and its corresponding policies should be kept.

If a promotion targeted at corporate clients of a hotel has been marginally successful, it will be analyzed according to its merits and either modified or discontinued. If a new strategy is called for, perhaps a sales promotion of giving an umbrella with the company's logo to corporate guests who stay over for one weekend night, it will be incrementally added to existing strategies. This is essentially saying that the vast majority of strategies, with some modifications, will remain the same. Marketing strategies, because of their dependence on the environment, are the functional area most subject to change. The majority of other functional areas will normally focus on improvements in execution.

Corporative politics: A common occurrence in strategy selection is that executives enter into the process with preconceived strategic agendas and are simply searching for compatible opportunities that support their biased views. This attitude negates the purpose of the planning process. Each participant must be open enough to realize that as new information comes to light, new strategies may be required. Plans must be based on valid information, not just opinion or one's position on the organization chart.

One common characteristic of corporate politics is that the lower one is in the corporate hierarchy, the more factual support must be presented when expressing views or opinions on possible strategies. This is a legitimate requirement in that those who are new to the business world will have fewer experiences to draw from when analyzing SWOT factors. "Great ideas" from young managers without proper research and support will seldom attract more than passing attention.

Viability of strategic alternatives

The remainder of the strategic analysis questions focus on the advantages, disadvantages, and viability of the strategic options and, finally, the most preferred options.

6. Are the strategic alternatives compatible with the firm's competitive environment?

The perceived opportunity must be based on factual data and a realistic appraisal of the situation, not on management's subjective speculation. If a strategy calls for improved quality at a higher price, customers must want higher quality and be willing to pay for it.

An occasional problem for independent fast-food restaurant operators is that they generally offer a higher quality product and charge more than chain fast-food operations. If this is what the customer demands, there is no problem, but if the restaurant's target customers resist higher prices for similar menu items, then it will need to find a way of reducing the price or increasing the perceived value of the meal. If a hotel company decides to build smaller, but luxurious, hotel rooms that will be offered at a mid-scale price, it must be sure there are enough customers who have a need for a less expensive, luxury hotel room. A problem with this strategy could be that the majority of guests desiring higher quality or luxury hotel rooms work for companies that pay for the room. Therefore, they may not be motivated by the opportunity to save money.

On the other hand, if there is a limited supply of the smaller rooms-less competition-then even if the demand is low, a niche (small protected market) might be available. If the firm had an experienced marketing staff-a strength-it might be possible through personal selling to contact companies with travel needs that would like to reduce their travel expenditures.

Timing. A key factor related to environmental compatibility is timing. Is the timing right for any certain course of action that may be selected? One of the goals of strategic market management is to be proactive seeing an opportunity or threat before others and taking advantage of it. Though generally a benefit of strategic planning, it can also cause severe problems. If a company acts too soon, thinking it will be a leader in an untapped market, the result may not be pleasant. Everyone knows what happened to many of the pioneers crossing the plains. For many strategies there may be a window of opportunity.

A strategy executed during this time might be successful; afterward, the risk goes up. A popular sand which chain was purchased from its creators in the early 1980s. People inquiring about purchasing franchises were told that none were going to be sold until the company was reorganized. At this time their part of the country was experiencing rapid growth with expansion in almost all business segments.

Unfortunately, the reorganization took several years and by the time the company was ready to sell franchises again, this region of the country was in recession, and few buyers were available.

An additional problem was that while the firm was stagnant, another sandwich chain penetrated the local markets, making expansion even more difficult. Also in the 1980s, D'Lites, a small chain of health-oriented fast-food hamburger restaurants, opened.

Because of the great initial curiosity on the part of consumers, many restaurants were opened within a short period of time. Once the novelty wore off and the company was not able to cover its debt, stores quickly began closing. Several imitators of this company also closed. They were trying to pioneer a concept before its time. Although customers were requesting healthier foods, only a small number were willing to change their present eating habits.

A related issue that will be garnering much strategic thought is the subject of smoking. At some point in the future it is likely that smoking will be banned from all public access buildings. Until this law is passed, there will be a great many people trying to minimize their exposure to smoke.

Many hotels and most restaurants have rooms or areas that are designated as nonsmoking. This has made these establishments more attractive to those who do not wish to be exposed to smoke. If a hotel or restaurant prohibits smoking altogether before a law is passed requiring it, are there enough nonsmokers to replace current smokers? Also, will smokers continue to frequent these establishments in spite of their self-imposed prohibition? Before a hospitality company adopts the strategy of prohibiting smoking, it must make sure that the timing is right.

7. Does the strategy place realistic demands on the abilities of the firm?

This requires an objective appraisal of the firm's strengths and weaknesses. A key opportunity can rarely be taken advantage of without a compatible strength with which it can be paired. For example, if consumer research indicates the need to upgrade the quality of food or service, or if a more demanding customer is added to the target customer base, then correspondingly greater skills in cooking, service, purchasing, and quality control will be necessary.

If a hotel company sees an opportunity to expand and desires to do so, financial resources, profit stability, operational systems, and adequate key personnel will be among the requisite skills. If customers are seeking value, and the firm has a low profit margin, it may not be in a position to effectively take advantage of the opportunity without major operational changes.

If a skill that is needed to take advantage of an attractive opportunity does not exist—a weakness—then management must decide whether it is worth the effort to make appropriate changes. An important skill related to the implementation of any strategy is the firm's current ability to effectively and consistently execute policies and action plans. If most activities of the business are already carried out according to standardized policies, then implementation and control of new policies or strategies will normally be simplified.

8. Is the strategy worth pursuing?

First and most important are the answers to the following questions: What are the financial or other competitive advantages, such as cost reductions (productivity), sales increases, improvement in image/ public relations, quality and employee relations benefits, that will accrue from the strategy?. What are the potential benefits of a $20,000 ad campaign for a mid-sized restaurant chain? Based on historical information and knowledge of the market, what might be the increase in sales during the campaign? Is the quality of the campaign such that it will have a residual effect either on sales or on the firm's image? Is the campaign a necessary evil to defend against a strong competitor? Would another strategy, such as targeting existing customers through internal merchandising, be more lucrative, easier to implement, and less of a risk? Can the costs involved in the campaign be reduced through co-promotions with vendors or other restaurants or hotels, limiting ad agency input, or sponsoring a charitable event? Are the risks involved acceptable, and what might be the likely results from pursuing a, certain strategy? Obviously, the hope is that something positive will result, but this is often based on some degree of optimism-blind or factually based. Generally, there is a double-barreled decision to be made. If 100 rooms are added, what could happen? On the other hand, if the 100 rooms are not added, what might happen to business? Customers may go elsewhere. There will always be risks involved in pursuing an opportunity, but there may often be greater risks involved in ignoring it.

9. How will competitors react?

A business must consider whether a competing firm will react to any specific strategic choice. If so, how soon, will it happen, what might that reaction be, what amount of effort will be brought to bear on it, and how could it affect the firm and its new strategies? Some industry segments react quickly to competitive moves, while others react slowly, if at all. The majority of competitive reactions in the hospitality business are instigated by a competing firm's promotion of new products and services or reductions in price for popular offerings.

In the convenience or economy segment of the market-fast-food and budget or limited-service hotels and motels-most counter strategies are related to changes in a competitor's price or other means of promoting prices, such as value meals. The reason for this is that since there is often a lack of differentiation between these competitors-the products and services are so similar that brand loyalty is low-the customer will quickly change buying habits according to who has the best deal.

As we learned from Porter's forces of competition that, in some instances, the customers have more power than the business, so they can dictate terms. When one fast-food restaurant lowers its price, primary and even secondary competitors are generally quick to follow. The alternative is a loss of market share or sales. There are, of course, instances where a fast-food restaurant's promotion of new menu items brings a reaction, but so far in the 1990s value promotions appear to garner the quickest response.

Pricing counterstrategies for midscale and luxury markets are much less obvious and are rarely used in promotional campaigns. Each firm will keep up with competitors' room prices and menu prices and utilize this information when making seasonal or scheduled price changes. Competitors' reactions in the midscale to upscale markets generally involve either a response to the addition of menu items or services, an increased emphasis on general advertising, or a focus on expansion.

Any type of promotional campaign that could affect a primary competitor's sales should take into account possible responses. The degree of potential effect, between minimal and severe, will generally match the competitor's reaction. Any such campaign should generally be accompanied by a contingency plan focused on defending against possible counterstrategies, especially attack or comparison advertisements. In many cases, this response would be a continued focus on the original campaign. For example, a hotel promoting its friendly service to the point of positioning itself as the "friendly hotel" would probably want to continue the promotion. As the competitor tries some type of diversion for the customer, through comparison ads or otherwise, the continued focus on friendly service during the battle would reinforce the attribute in the customer's mind.

Of course, there is always the possibility that a competitor might develop an extremely effective comparison ad campaign that belittles the firm's "friendly service" ads. If this occurs, it is up to the marketing department to outgun the competitor with a direct response, begin working on another positive ad campaign, or lay low for a time to avoid an expensive promotional battle. A common strategy by most large hospitality firms is that of expanding locations in order to be number one in a market. The possible counterstrategies are to select other markets or, if the market in question is strategic, to follow a competing firm's expansion strategy in an attempt to limit its ability to achieve the competitive advantage of being number one in a market.

Probable strategic direction

10. Mat should be the primary strategic thrusts for the next planning period?

After pertinent SWOT factors or groups of SWOT factors have been analyzed and potentially viable strategic alternatives have been selected, probable strategic thrusts and the general direction that new strategies will take are decided on. The purpose of this, as with the rest of the strategic analysis process, is to increase the likelihood of an objective diagnosis of key issues and a platform from which to discuss remaining components of the strategic plan. It is not imperative at this point that selected strategic thrusts be set in stone. Through the questioning process many advantages and disadvantages will have been considered, but more will come forth as the planning process continues. Strategic thrusts can be a single strategic alternative, such as "Promote more weekend packages"; or a combination of strategies that focus on increasing promotions, such as "Increase the promotional budget." This might include strategy alternatives, such as the above promotion of more weekend packages, increasing the use of radio, adding in-flight and meeting planner magazines to the promotional mix, doubling spending on the secretary's club, and so forth.

The strategic analysis questioning process provides planners with a methodical means of determining key situational variables and potential strategies. This planning step not only saves time, as objectives and various functional strategies are set, but also improves the effectiveness of the overall planning effort. No planning process or model will ever detail specifically what must be done to assure success, but attempts must be made at clarifying these complicated decisions and improving results. In the end, management must simply gather the best possible information, analyze it in an organized logical manner, and then make a decision.

Strategic marketing is the set of basic actions the company will follow to achieve its long-term objectives and to serve the long-term demands of the market. The primary goals of strategic marketing for a single business are (1) to maximize the firm's position within its chosen markets by establishing a clear distinction between its offering and that of competitors; (2) to determine what factors are necessary for the firm to attain its strongest position; (3) to allow the firm to specialize in an area where it can either be the best of its competitive segment or one of the best; (4) to provide marketing managers with a target on which their efforts can be focused; and (5) to continuously learn from experience and seek ways of improving the firm's position.

The primary focus of strategic marketing is on grand strategies, the decisions concerning the products and services that will be offered, the market or markets for which the firm will compete, and the timing of any new product/service introductions or market additions. These strategies are critical because they are what the business will be known for-what it sells and to whom it sells it. There are normally very few major changes in a firm's grand strategies, but there may well be many minor ones. For example, a midscale hotel will rarely upgrade to the luxury market, but it may add new customer or market segments, find new means of promoting to existing customers, renovate the hotel, or add new products or services. Sometimes marketers will begin to consider how the marketing mix variables (product, price, place, and promotion) will be used to support the grand strategy. However, this task is normally determined later in the planning process.

Concurrently with the setting of grand strategies, the firm should examine the extend to which generic strategies, product life cycles, portfolio analysis, and factors related to its industry position should be incorporated into the grand strategies.

There is no explicit time frame for strategic marketing plans. They are essentially the plans for the long-term future of the business. The time frame for the plan and its implementation will vary by need and importance.

Some areas of the strategic plan will be focused on the immediate future; others will be planned for several years in the future. If it is decided in the strategic plan that menu changes reflecting lower fat entrees are needed now, then objectives, marketing strategies (or any other functional area), and action plans will begin detailing their immediate implementation.

If management feels that the change will not be necessary for three years, then it will be noted in the strategic plan, and applicable long-term objectives will be set with little further attention until managerial actions are necessary to prepare for implementation. If changes in the environment occurred that would affect the long-term strategy, then the time frame or the strategy could be altered or simply not implemented. Some companies, especially those that anticipate vast expansion, may have several time frames, such as for the next five, ten, and fifteen years in the future.

The strategic plans are often general, such as to add new services to remain competitive and to satisfy existing target customers. The method of achieving the above longterm strategy would best be included in the functional strategies section. For example, begin offering room service until 12 midnight, and add a workout room with professional equipment. The details of their implementation would be included later in the marketing action plan.

Grand strategies

There are two primary categories of grand strategies: intensive and extensive (normally referred to as diversification). These are sometimes known as growth strategies, because they focus on growth within the firm's current products and markets or growth in related or unrelated businesses.

As any of these possible strategic actions are incorporated into the firm's strategic marketing plan, marketing managers will need to decide which of the specific marketing mix variables (product, price, place, and promotion) will be used to accomplish them. If, for example, it was decided that a new market (intensive growth) will be added, then perhaps new or modified products or services at an acceptable price must be adopted, the product must be in the right place (distribution channel or location), and the changes must then be promoted (communicated) to the new market segment.

The marketing mix variables in this context are referred to as strategies because they help guide the strategic direction of the firm. Here, they are used in the general sense, by stating that a certain strategy, a pricing strategy, for example, will be used to help achieve the grand strategies. The specifics of how they will be used are known as marketing action plans or, in generic planning terms, tactics, which describe exactly how they will be carried out in the next planning period. This explanation must be made because in various marketing textbooks the marketing mix variables are described as either strategies or tactics, or as both strategies and tactics. Each of these uses is correct based on the author's interpretation. What is critical is not what they are called, but how they are used to increase the effectiveness of the firm's planning efforts.

Intensive strategies

Intensive strategies are concerned with improving the performance of existing businesses. They focus on various internal means of retaining and expanding the firms' market share or sales. Most activities will relate to increasing the frequency of present customers, increasing their average amount spent, or attracting new customers.

1 . Concentration or penetration-focusing on the current market with the current product
2. Product and service development-focusing on the new products and services targeted at existing markets
3. Market development-focusing on new markets.

Concentration or penetration

For existing products and services in existing markets, this basically means selling more of present products or services to the existing customer base, or simply doing a better job of what is currently being done. The key advantage of concentration is that the company is doing what it does best-dealing with known competencies. It knows its product and market, and knows what works and what does not. One disadvantage of concentration is that a company can become lulled into inactivity or complacency by not focusing on changes in the environment. If a company becomes overconfident in its present product or service mix, it may lose touch with shifts in demand and suffer dearly for it later. For example, for many years McDonald's concentrated on a limited product line, and average-to-high prices relative to competitors.

As consumers' tastes changed and pocketbooks were squeezed, McDonald's sat by, watching as competitors adapted. They changed only after Taco Bell's value-focused menu garnered a substantial increase in sales and market share. For many years Holiday Inn controlled the middle market in the hotel industry. In the 1970s that market began breaking up into smaller segments. Holiday Inn did not respond to these changes and saw competitors like La Quinta and Days Inn take a major share of its market.

Being on automatic pilot or doing what was done in

the past is acceptable for brief periods of time. But changing times require changes in the fundamental offerings of firms, and this necessitates the consideration of improvements in current products and services, or the development of new products and services, or the addition of new markets. If new locations were opened in the same city, in trade areas with similar target customers, the strategy could still be considered penetration-trying to sell more to existing customers.

The firm is trying to penetrate its market. If new locations were opened in new cities, the strategy would generally be considered market development. When locations in the same city are opened in trade areas with significantly different target customers, it would be best to refer to it as market development. The purpose for this is to increase management's focus on matching existing product with the new market. When very serious problems exist or there is an opportunity to sell the business at a profit the strategies of turnaround, divestment, or liquidation should be considered.

— *Turnaround*. When a major effort is required to correct the downward direction of sales, profits, or operational performance a form of concentration strategy referred to as a turnaround should be implemented. In this situation, everything must be viewed as suspect, but in most such circumstances there will be pockets of good mixed in with the major problems. In one turnaround situation, two weeks of management training and the simple elimination of wasted advertising expenditures resulted in a 10% turnaround in profit. If a turnaround is neither successful nor feasible, then perhaps the entire business or parts of it should be sold.

— *Divestment*. Sell the business as an ongoing concern. In all but the rarest circumstances, it is best for a business to be sold while it is operating rather than when it is closed. If sales volume for a restaurant is terrible, then it may be best to close to minimize losses. Because of the extraordinary issues in maintaining a closed hotel, such as cost of security, vandalism, and mildew, it is uncommon for a hotel to close.

— *Liquidation.* Sell the business in parts. This could be a large hotel or restaurant company selling off one or more of its properties. It most often refers to the selling off of components of a business, such as the hotel or restaurant building company or selling furniture, fixtures, and equipment.

Concentration strategies and total quality management (TQM)

Quality makes it possible for the customer to have a love affair with your product. Buzzwords come and go, but perhaps one of the most beneficial concepts in modern business history is total quality management (TQM). It is defined as "a structured process for establishing long-range goals, at the highest levels of organization, and defining the means to be used to reach those goals". This structured process refers to quality planning, quality control, and quality improvement. Quality in relation to business has been defined in different ways but can generally be expressed as satisfying the customer's expectations, or simply keeping the customer happy. Inherent in this definition is consistency, a term not lost on longterm high achievers in the hospitality industry.

The drive for quality has been so intense in recent years that customers are beginning to expect quality in everything they buy. Companies not joining in are watching their customer bases quickly erode. Spender tells us that "excellence, vision, commitment, teamwork, and service have recaptured the attention of top management." The implicit ramifications of a quality product or service are increased frequency of use or habitual purchases and exponential increases in word-of-mouth advertising.

Except for variable costs, much of the increased business volume goes directly to the bottom line. Another benefit of TQM has been increased productivity. The service sector has not enjoyed the productivity returns realized by the manufacturing industries, primarily because of its high labor intensity. Much of what has been written on TQM has focused on the manufacturing sectors. This has occurred for two reasons: (1) the decline in America's manufacturing dominance and (2) the increased ease of measuring and controlling the production of a product as opposed to a service.

The 1970s brought the realization that products manufactured in America were no longer the standard against which the world's products were measured. The decline first became apparent in the automotive industry, then was closely followed by almost every conceivable product. The service sector was somewhat insulated by the fact that it was more difficult to penetrate the hotel and restaurant markets than manufacturing or product markets. Panicking companies scouring the world for the answer to decreased market share found it in an increased respect for quality. What was astonishing is that the key proponents and theorists of quality, W. Edwards Deming and J.M. Juran, had been trumpeting its importance since the 1920s, but their pleas had fallen on deaf ears. The problem in America was that there was plenty of business to go around, so few companies were concerned enough to listen and learn. Both Deming and Juran found their most enthusiastic audiences in Japan. As "Made in Japan" changed from being a symbol of cheap workmanship to one of excellence, and American market shares dwindled, American firms were forced to listen.

The reasons American firms have fallen behind much of the world in the area of quality are numerous, but a businessman from Japan had the following observation. He said that in the Asian culture, sensitivity to other people guides their proclivity for quality. Americans tend to focus on what is good for themselves, thereby neglecting details and quality. It appears that American companies respond to quality only when red ink replaces black ink.

As gains developed from TQM and processes became standardized, service sector firms began attempting to adopt its principles. They soon found that measurement of service quality was much more difficult than product quality. While products are quite tangible and can be measured by defects per hundred thousand or million, service is an intangible whose performance is based on customer and management perception.

Additionally, this perception varied among each customer and manager, based on geographic, demographic, psychographic, and behavioral characteristics. Some measurements were possible, such as check-out time or the average time necessary for the kitchen to process a food order, but this did not present a complete picture of how the company was doing.

To improve the transferability of TQM from manufacturing to service sectors, hotel and foodservice companies had to find alternative means of measuring quality. This fact has led to an increased use of customer surveys to find answers to questions on such things as what customers thought of the level of quality of their services, differences between the customer's expectations and perceptions, how often they returned, and how often they bought from competitors.

Survey information was then incorporated into all segments of the business. Proactive companies began taking a daily measure of customer satisfaction and taking immediate action to correct problems before they become endemic to the business.

Management realized that it was not they but their employees who were responsible for assuring customer satisfaction. In fact, for most service companies, the lower an employee is on the organizational chart, the greater his/her impact on quality. With this acknowledgment came an increased focus on empowering employees to do whatever is necessary to make sure that the customer is satisfied.

Total quality management programme: The steps for developing and implementing a TQM program for the hospitality industry are essentially the same as those of strategic marketing.

1. *Find out what product and service attributes are judged to be important by the customers*. Also, find out what factors are considered important to employees, stockholders, and other stakeholders. Rank each attribute or factor based on how important each is to the success of the business.

2. *Determine how the company is presently performing in each area*. A common recommendation of TQM practitioners is to locate the company's biggest problems and begin by focusing all efforts there first. A version of this approach is to locate and begin solving the most serious problems in each functional area of the business. The easiest place to begin for line workers is to start with the big picture. Have them create a flowchart detailing their movement when performing their jobs. This helps give them a simple place to start their analysis.

One of the keys to identifying performance deviations is that management must have some means of statistically measuring the performance of key tasks, especially those that affect customers or are considered critical to their satisfaction. Without measurement, control is relegated to the inconsistency of qualitative and subjective opinions. This is a not a totally negative circumstance, but is less accurate.

Measurement for line workers is often easier than for management personnel. To measure management efficiency, begin by deciding what a particular manager's most important responsibility is. Then calculate how much of his/her time is spent on that task and other less important tasks. If too much time is spent on tasks that do not improve quality—for example, paperwork or excessive meetings—then those impediments to better performance should be removed.

3. *Set objectives that will lead to incremental improvement in areas where present performance is not at an acceptable level.* Objectives should be as detailed as possible and follow the categories of social responsibility, profitability, productivity, employee development, employee relations, competitive position, and technology. One method of deciding on how high to set objectives, and in exactly which areas to set them, is to use the performance of excellent companies as a benchmark. The company should be careful not to set objectives too high or to focus on too many areas at once. Luckily it is much easier for hospitality firms, to make quantum leaps in quality than it is for manufacturing firms. The manufacturing firm may require months of retooling and redesigning of products, while hospitality firms can with much less effort change a few policies, retrain, and motivate employees to meet the new standards.

4. *Decide what strategies will most effectively lead to the achievement of objectives.* It is critical for management to not only include line employees and middle management in the process, but to give them the responsibility and authority to make reasonable changes in operating procedures. Once employees are effectively trained and rewarded, and supervisors are coaching employees to keep their performance in line with objectives, then the company should be on its way to major improvements in quality.

There are various terms used for attracting employee input in the decisionmaking process: quality circles, task teams, and self-managing work teams. Each offers a successively greater degree of employee control over the work environment.

Quality circles are groups of employees doing similar or related work who meet regularly to identify and analyze means of improving their input into the overall quality of the firm's product or service. Their popularity has been losing ground because employees are not given much guidance as to the problems that need to be addressed and their input is not always considered by management when deciding on necessary change. Task teams are similar to quality circles, except they are given relatively explicit directions as to what they should focus on. Self-managing work teams are given the responsibility of total control over their portion of operations (line) or support (staff) process. They have control over all tasks for which they are responsible, including the setting of schedules and division of assignments.

5. *Institutionalizing the new strategies.* A number of companies have looked upon TQM as a series of operational steps that lead to excellence, but it generally involves an overhaul of the organization's

corporate culture, structure, style of leadership, and reward systems. From the president down to the lowest paid employee, everyone must buy into the company's quest for quality. Few people readily accept change. TQM must be sold to employees just as the company sells its product to customers. Each target group of employees must be analyzed to determine the best method of introducing necessary changes. Of course, if employees were to help develop the new strategies and policies, cooperation would be much more likely. Additionally, some type of system should be in place to reward workers for improvement.

6. *Postimplementation efforts.* Monitor performance for deviation from objectives. Ideally, all employees should have their efforts measured daily Keeping the employees aware of how they are doing in critical performance areas lets them know what the company considers to be important. When corrections are necessary, update policies and action plans.

The key to successful quality control in the hospitality industry is to build the philosophy of quality into the operational system and corporate culture of the business. This is accomplished through management's enthusiasm and support for the program's policies and its recognition of employees when objectives are reached.

Most employees want to do a good job and are proud of their efforts; they simply need to be shown what constitutes a quality performance and to be recognized for it. The company's efforts, both good and bad, should be regularly discussed at employee meetings, during evaluations, and during everyday supervision. Ideally, TQM should be viewed as a worthy challenge to employees. The goal is to increase the entrepreneurial spirit of employees by showing them that reaching objectives is good for both them and the company.

Pitfalls of TQM: Too often executives voice their concern for the importance of quality, but their personal actions or managerial style do not provide the foundation for a quality-directed effort. A TQM program requires much more than saying quality is important, then waiting for employees to make quality happen. It entails a detailed set of plans and actions that must be integrated into every part of the organization. Before a firm initiates a total quality management program, it should be aware of the pitfalls that may be encountered both before and during implementation.

1. *False starts.* Total quality management (or strategic marketing) takes time. Often, executives will get people overly excited about the new changes, then, because of the length of the process, will not get back with them for months. In the meantime, employees' initial enthusiasm drops, and they become cynical about the effort.

2. *Disconnection from customer issues.* An excellent quality product or service may be worthless if it is not what the customer wants. Close customer contact and feedback are required for total quality, because the firm must determine how it is currently doing, plus be aware of new demands.

3. *"Do" Versus "Develop."* W. Edwards Deming's framework for managing and implementing total quality focuses on four phases: (a) a plan for improvement is created; (b) the plan is put into effect; (c) during implementation, checkpoints are monitored and adjustments made; and (d) when all the fine-tuning is completed, the final phase is to freeze the process and continuously improve it. In Japan, the emphasis is on phases (a) and (c), because they are

aggressive in determining whether or not their plan is on course.

4. *"We're Doing Okay."* Frequently, businesses feel that if profits are good, then quality is good. The Malcolm Baldrige National Quality Award has a requirement that quality be integrated into all activities and be an overriding concern for all decisions. Donald E. Petersen, former chairman of Ford Motor Company, said, "The principle by which we live and die is that, once we do something well, we have to figure out how to do it even better." David Kearns, chairman of Xerox Corporation, echoed this idea when he started, "As we get better, so does our competition. We are in a race for which there is no finish line."
5. *The quick-fix syndrome.* Normally, quality problems cannot be corrected quickly. Since the development of a new process that allows for continuous improvement may take several weeks or months, results may not be immediately apparent.
6. *Mandate and move on.* Executives frequently implement a quality program, then neglect it to focus on other things. Total quality management requires that managers assume an active, hands-on role.
7. *No space on the agenda.* Executives must master the skills necessary to implement a quality program. U.S. executives spend an average of 40% of their time on routine matters and 60% solving problems, Winners of Japan's Deming Prize for quality spend 20% of their time on routine work, 20% on problems, and 60% on actions that lead to continuous quality improvement.
8. *Look who's running the show.* Since it is generally necessary to put someone in charge of the business's quality effort, someone whose past work exemplifies quality should be selected.

9. *No guts at crunch time.* When the pressure is on to reach financial objectives, the quality effort must not be put on the back burner.

The three costs of quality: As successful strategies necessitate proactive planning, so does quality control. The causes of quality control problems should be found and their solutions built into routine activities. At the root of quality control issues are the related costs of quality. According to Labovitz and Chang, costs can be divided into three areas:

1. *Prevention costs—good costs.* Costs of quality are "good" if they relate to preventing mistakes that affect product costs and customer complaints. It is always preferable to prevent a problem before it occurs than to correct it afterward. Examples of prevention costs are effective hiring policies; quality-conscious personnel; training and supervision that focus on supporting quality-oriented standards; and tying compensation, evaluations, and promotions to quality performance.

2. *Inspection and correction costs—bad costs.* Obviously, inspection and correction in the hospitality business will always be a primary component of a supervisor's job. A dilemma arises because even though it is good to find and correct the problem, this is only a short-term solution and, unfortunately, it must be repeated over and over. The objective here is to minimize the amount of time spent on locating and solving problems, especially those that occur frequently. This allows a greater focus on the customer and other more productive endeavors. If a hotel's general manager is having trouble with food cost, high labor costs, and a less-than-friendly front-desk staff, these are symptoms of a greater problem-the failure to allocate time and money for prevention costs.

3. *Customer complaints—ugly costs.* If prevention or inspection and correction do not stop substandard performance, customer complaints are the result. It is important that the business apologize for its mistakes, but it would be much better off if it avoided them instead. Since word-of-mouth advertising is the most important means of communicating a product offering to customers, negative word-of mouth must be avoided at all costs.

Labovitz and Chang also developed the "1-10-100 Rule" to compare the three costs of quality. Basically, every $1 spent in prevention costs (good) will save the company $10 in inspection and correction costs (bad) and $100 in customer complaint costs (ugly). Obviously, this is an approximation, but it does emphasize the relative importance of each cost of quality.

Product and service development

This category includes the development of new or modified products or services for existing customers. There will always be a need to consider what new products and services will be demanded in the future. Most companies will concentrate primarily on their existing product offering, then have a constant ongoing search for potential new products. Most often, product or service additions are modifications of existing offerings. If competition is fierce or the product or service has reached the end of its life cycle, then an entirely new or innovative product or service may be needed.

Technically, this definition uses the broad interpretation of "existing customer," such as customers of fast-food restaurants or guests of a luxury hotel. However, in the hospitality business, the categorization of product development as new products and services for existing customers is not always used in this manner. This is because when a business adds a new product or service, it may also add customers from other market segments as well.

For example, if a restaurant adds fresh vegetables, a salad bar, or a new category to a menu, such as seafood, existing customers may appreciate the change and return more often, but a parallel result is that is will likely bring in new customer segments. How many will depend on the degree of divergence from the existing offering and individual variances within existing customer segments.

If a fast-food restaurant adds mushrooms and avocado to a burger, existing customers may purchase it or come back more frequently for it, but it may also attract a new customer segment in search of a better tasting, higher quality, or more regionally acceptable burger.

If the same restaurant adds a grilled chicken breast sandwich and a selection of salads, then a new segment will almost certainly be added. If a hotel adds a workout room, it will have the objective of increasing the loyalty of existing customers, but it may also bring in customers, however small the number, from other market segments.

A hotel adding computerized check-in and check-out and business services would generally be focusing on product and service development in the technical sense. It would simply be allowing the hotel to better meet the demands of the current target market. But if this hotel were in the midscale market, such as a Holiday Inn, it may also have an eye on adding customers from the bottom end of the upper midscale market-customer's that stay at Hiltons and Marriotts but who may temporally or permanently be on a tight budget.

When a fine dining restaurant or luxury hotel adds almost any product or service to its products or service mix, this could be considered product development in the strictest sense, because these firms generally have only one target market and are not usually concerned about attracting other segments.

When the goal of new products or services is specifically to bring in new market segments, some planners will use the term diversification or, more properly, intensive diversification (i.e., a new product and a new market). In most cases, if a firm wanted to add new products, it would be appropriate to use the terms product development and diversification interchangeably (e.g., "diversify our product offering"). Perhaps a better definition of product development would be researching and developing new products and services with the primary purpose of increasing brand loyalty of existing customers, the secondary purpose being the attraction of new market segments. In any case, the terminology used is secondary to application.

Market development

This includes selling existing products to new customer segments—market segment development—or to customers in anew location—geographic market development. The need for market segment development will vary greatly depending on the dynamics of the business's customer base. Most businesses will have the same primary target customers each year but will find permanent or temporary opportunities in secondary target customer groups. A business could add primary customer segments, such as catering, meeting, or banquet services, or try to attract senior citizens, college students, those who are willing to pay more for their meals or rooms, or guests who will stay for a week or longer.

Subsegments of the business's target segments could be added with minor modifications of existing strategies, such as products, services, prices, atmosphere, or promotion. Improving a hotels' workout facility, adding heart-healthy items to the menu, and promoting these changes may attract health-oriented customers within the hotel's present individual business traveler market segment. Decisions related to adding new customer segments are based on information from customer segmentation research and market-targeting decisions.

Market targeting: The primary purpose of segmentation is to learn enough about the various segments of the market to be able to determine which will have the potential to become viable target markets. Effective targeting is the result of an adequate base of information concerning the personal characteristics of the target customers. This will allow the business not only to select the appropriate markets but also to more effectively position its products and services for that market.

Most firms will have one or more primary target markets, possibly some subsegments within primary markets, and secondary target markets. Because of limited returns, secondary markets do not generally attract a great deal of the marketing department's attention or time. Far too many firms assume that what their customers wanted last year is what they will want this year. Often this is true, but when changes do occur, the firm that realizes it first and takes the appropriate action has the opportunity to reap substantial benefits.

Selecting target markets: A decision must be made on whether or not to target one market, a new markets, or several markets. Single-market targeting allows the firm to focus on just one market, and therefore to maximize valuable resources and its opportunities. The problem with focusing on a single market is that changes in the market will have a proportionately greater effect on a business that adopts this approach than on firms that rely on several market segments. There is also a tendency for firms to drift into complacency and become aware of changes in demand only when it is too late.

Firms using the single-segment targeting strategy should do so only with the knowledge that they are the best (or one of the best) alternative for their targeted group. An additional reason for deciding on a single segment is the location of a niche that can be protected, or that is likely to be ignored by others. This strategy has been particularly effective with upscale restaurants and luxury hotels. In the future, because of broad societal and demographic shifts and increased competition for each market, single-market targeting will most likely increase in importance.

Selective targeting, or targeting a limited number of markets, expands the business's opportunities and limits its dependence on a single market. It gives the firm the option and flexibility of going after multiple segments to fill rooms and restaurant seats during off-peak times. Selective targeting essentially allows the firm to maximize its market penetration while remaining focused on only a few specific segments.

Extensive targeting, or full marketing coverage, is attempting to gain a large market share by targeting the majority of the potential users of one's products or services. This mass-market targeting strategy can be approached from two perspectives:

1. *Differentiated market targeting*. The Marriott hotel chain could not satisfy all customers with its upper-midscale hotels. It was also reaching a saturation point in many geographic markets. The strategy it selected was differentiated market targeting developing different concepts for each market segment within a product or service category. Most of the major hotel chains are

pursuing this strategy because it allows them to maximize their brand's image, sales, and synergy in many functional areas, such as reservations, advertising, and operations.

2. *Undifferentiated market targeting*. The focus of firms utilizing undifferentiated marketing is to offer one product or service to all market segments. The objective of this targeting strategy is to reduce costs by focusing on larger markets. The problem is that larger markets often attract well-financed, established firms that are relentlessly attempting to hang onto market share. Since few businesses can satisfy broad segments of a product's market, it is generally best to either reduce one's scope with the use of selective targeting, or to expand one's offerings with the use of differentiated market targeting.

Requirements for target markets: Since not all segments will have the same potential, some means of analyzing each segment must be used to decide which of them to enter. The target customer segments identified for a restaurant or hotel can evaluated according to the following criteria:

— *Measurable*. Each segment chosen must be measurable by components of the four bases of segmentation, such as number of people in the segment, zip code, income, age, life-style activities, frequency of use, and price sensitivity. Companies that do not measure their markets tend to focus on either mass markets or ill-defined target markets.

— *Substantial*. The segment must be large enough to be worthwhile pursuing. The focus for most businesses will be their largest potential markets. Occasionally, as subsegment of a market or a secondary market may be substantial enough to pursue, as long as the business realizes that it probably cannot expect sizable returns. If the smaller market has been ignored, then this could be considered a niche that could be exploited. Secondary markets include college students, senior citizens, salespeople with small firms, or construction workers who travel for their companies.

— *Profitability*. Since profit is the driving force behind business, marketing managers must be confident that selected target markets both want and will purchase their product at a satisfactory price. Profitability will normally be estimated based on actions of existing target customers or through researching the experience of other firms.

— *Product differentiation*. The segments selected should allow for maximum differentiation between a company and its competitors. Differentiation can be defined as brand awareness and loyalty based on attributes such as product or service quality, atmosphere, cleanliness, past advertising, image, locations, and value. This term usually refers to positive differences that customers feel are important in the selection of one business over another. If management does not feel that it can compete head-on with its primary competitors with a similar product and price, then it must continue its search for a market that will value its offering. If the market does not see a noticeable difference between two products, then brand recognition and loyalty will be a primary influence on the purchasing decision.

For example, it would probably be unwise for an independently owned casual hamburger restaurant to open up in the same trade areas as a Chili's restaurant, unless it has something that differentiates its offering from Chili's—perhaps an in-store bakery exhibition kitchen, more seafood than Chili's, or a very popular signature dish.

Management should also try to find market gaps or niches in the market-needs that are not currently being met. In the ideal situation, the gap or niche represents an area of the market that can to some degree be protected or that will be ignored by primary competitors. These gaps could be in any areas that represent the potential for increases in sales or business expansion, such as location, atmosphere, price, concept (e.g., fast-food restaurant or economy hotel), menu items, and services. For example, the only sandwich shop in a trade area with a high percentage of office workers finds out that pizza is the only lunch item available for delivery. If customers are receptive to ordering sandwiches for delivery, then a potentially profitable, measurable, and accessible gap in the market has been located.

— *Accessible*. Either the target customer must be accessible to the business, through being in the business's trade area, or, if the business must rely on promotional activities, promotional options must be available at a reasonable cost. Targeting decisions for restaurants revolve around customers in their trade area—the area immediately around the location where approximately 60% to 70% of its customers either live or work.

Obviously, the trade area for a hotel will be much larger, and therefore require a much more sophisticated promotional effort. Hotels at the budget end of the market will rely on travelers that are driving through their trade area. As their sophistication and promotional budget grow, they may become part of reservation systems such as SABRE, or the travel agents' Red Book, which will help promote the hotel to callers requesting hotel rooms. Most chain hotels will try to attract guests from the United States or internationally using their own reservation system. Each city will generally find that a dispro-portionately large percentage of its guests travel from only a few cities, states, or countries. For most hotels in Texas, other Texas cities supply the majority of guests. For a growing number of hotel chains, Mexico is an increasingly large target market. Many hotels in San Francisco will focus a substantially larger percentage of their promotional budget on the Far East than will hotels in most other U.S. cities.

— *Stable*. Decision-makers must be confident that the market will be around for a long enough period of time to allow for a reasonable return on the business's investment. If the investment is low, as when a restaurant adds a menu item that may be a fad, there is no major problem. If the investment concerns remodeling, expansion, or major strategies affecting the firm's products and service, pricing structure image or promotional campaign, marketers must be confident that the market will be there for the foreseeable future.

Geographic market development: This concerns opening new locations of the same business in other areas-generally other cities. The new geographic markets would normally be located and identified in the customer analysis, and occasionally in the competitor analysis.

Care must be taken not to expand too quickly out of one's area of strength. For restaurants, it is generally better to focus on penetrating a single geographic area first (existing customers in one's existing market) and then to expand to nearby areas. There are several reasons for this, First, as the succeeding locations are opened, they will be within arm's reach, so as problems arise, management can handle them quickly. Second, selecting a location in a city where owners and managers have lived for several years is much easier than finding a location in another city after a two-day visit.

Since the future of the business may depend on the

success of new geographic locations, it is best to prepare a detailed site analysis and to have someone from the company live on the site for about a week to see it under all possible conditions.

As expansion takes place in the business's present market, customers will recognize the name and, based on its good reputation, be much more likely to patronize the restaurant than one they have never heard of. For this same reason, once the decision has been made to expand out of one's current market, it is generally best to expand into the nearest suitable markets.

The question of expanding to new geographic markets for a hotel will largely depend on whether it gets the majority of its business from walk-ins or reservations. A new, quality-oriented roadside motel can open up in almost any new geographic area with satisfactory results, as long as it is located near similar successful motels.

Chain hotels with excellent name recognition and reservation systems can open a hotel in almost any location that is in need of more or newer rooms. Small chains or independents with limited name recognition should generally penetrate their current markets first, then focus expansion on nearby markets. Since expansion normally is derived from takeovers of other properties, there may be more emphasis placed on the "deal" than on the location.

Recently, when a relatively new five-unit hotel chain took over and reflagged a top brand hotel, the occupancy dropped 25%. It took one year for the hotel to increase volume to 10% below its predecessor. To a large degree, success will depend on how well management was able to limit overhead in the deal and on the aggressive work of their marketing department.

Diversification

Diversification concerns adding businesses that will increase the firm's competitive advantage. This could be through lowering costs, increasing quality, increasing market penetration, improving efficiency, raising sales, or increasing profits. Diversification generally refers to opening a new business outside the current business. When used in this context, it is more properly termed extensive diversification.

Categories include horizontal, concentric, and conglomerate diversification. Technically, it is either getting into a new business that is similar to the existing business, into one within the same industry but in a different segment, or into a new type of business altogether.

Colloquially, the term can also be used to connote adding a new product to an existing business. Each firm may have different meanings for diversification. The primary point is that everyone involved should understand the context in which the term is being used, so that functional strategies can be written that support the intended grand strategy.

One major study of 33 firms' efforts in diversification found that it was not usually an effective strategy. The measure of success of the diversification strategy was whether the acquired firm was retained or divested. In this particular study, the overall divestment rate was well over 50% of all acquisitions. It was also found that it was the lawyers, investment bankers, and original sellers that profited from the acquisition and consequent divestment of the subsidiaries.

Common problems with diversification are the following:

1. Competition occurs at the business unit not at the

corporate level. Therefore, corporate officers must either have experience with the acquired firm or be willing to relinquish responsibility to others.

2. Diversification can add cost and constraints to the acquired business units. For example, in most cases the acquired business will have to pay its share of its new corporate parent's overhead, There may also be corporate philosophies and cultures that differ from that of the new subsidiary.

3. Shareholders can diversify their own portfolios. Unless the acquired business adds value to the bottom line of the parent corporation in an amount that is greater than the two individual businesses, the shareholders would be better off purchasing the stock themselves. What happens in these acquisitions is that the parent company has maximized its growth in its base industry or has a significant amount of retained earnings and thinks that it can add value to its company with the acquisition.

Conditions for acquisition

Porter described the conditions by which true shareholder value could be created.

1. *Attractiveness test*. The broad structure of the industry of the acquisition must represent opportunities for the potential subsidiary. Often, there will be businesses that for one reason or another are not achieving their potential. If the parent firm has certain competencies that can help the potential acquisition maximize its competitive position, then a purchase could be considered.

2. *Cost-of-entry test*. The purchase price must allow for a reasonable return on investment (ROI). If the parent firm is not confident that future profits will amortize the investment, the purchase should not be considered.

3. *Better-off test*. The new business unit must bring the parent firm a competitive advantage or vice versa.

Horizontal classification

This category includes opening another business that competes for the same customer, or purchasing a primary competitor; essentially getting into a business in the same level of the marketing channel. Examples include a midscale hotel purchasing another midscale hotel, or a fast-food restaurant chain acquiring a competing fast-food chain.

Concentrated diversification

This involves the acquisition of a business that is related to the hospitality business or that would use similar skills. This could be through direct similarities or through common operating characteristics; for example, a restaurant buying a specialty grocery store. Horizontal diversification and vertical integration could be included in this category.

Conglomerate diversification

This category includes the purchase of unrelated businesses. This strategy rarely works because of the lack of synergy of skills. For example, someone who operates restaurants should probably stay away from the printing business.

Vertical integration

This consists of opening or purchasing a supplier to one's business—backward vertical integration—or purchasing an organization that is a customer to one's business—forward vertical integration. Although it does not happen very often, there are many ways of utilizing backward vertical integration, such as when a restaurant or hotel gets into the bakery, linen, or produce business or an equipment supply or service company. Several restaurants have had problems obtaining quality produce or seafood, so they bypassed their wholesaler and began buying directly from farmers and fishermen. Eventually, some began selling to other restaurants. Forward vertical integration in the hospitality business is not as common. Some examples would be a hotel purchasing a travel agency or reservation system that supplies it with customers and a franchise headquarters purchasing its franchisees.

Other grand strategies

Often, firms that want to pursue diversification or integration strategies do not have adequate funds or expertise. Common options include joint venture, strategic alliance, franchising, management contracts, and acquisitions and mergers. Joint venture is the combining of resources with another company for mutual benefit.

A strategic alliance occurs when a smaller company, generally with expertise, time, and little money, joins with a larger company with money or available credit, and a broad business background, including the opportunity to achieve a competitive advantage, such as an expanded reservation system.

Franchising is the licensing of others to operate a business using the firm's operating system and brand name. Management contracts include a variety of agreements between those that have the expertise and reputation for successfully operating a particular type of business and those that own the business.

Management contracts have become quite common in the lodging and institutional segments of the foodservice industry Though not widespread in restaurants, their use will likely increase in proportion to competitive intensity. Acquisitions are basically the outright purchase of another business that may continue to operate under its own name. Mergers occur when two or more firms are combined to create one firm.

Generic strategies

Generic strategies were designed to help guide the overall strategic selection process. The most popular generic strategy is that of Michael Porter. He proposed that the generic strategy typology of overall low-cost leadership, differentiation, and focus could be applied to any industry and that his accompanying theories would result in higher than average returns. He added that each firm should select one generic strategy to focus on and that the suitability of each would vary based on the industry's stage in its product life cycle. To this mix, other authors have added preemptive and synergy.

There is no doubt that these generic strategies have made a major impact on the science of business. And no one can argue with the fact that each if effectively pursued in the appropriate environment can lead to improvements in a firm's competitive standing. But in the context of strategy-setting, "What additions did they make to the strategists' tool box?" and "Can strategists rely on a relatively static generic strategy for deciding their business's future?" For example, all businesses know that they must keep costs as low as possible to remain competitive and that there must be some relative uniqueness about their product or service offering that attracts an adequate number of customers. Also, it is rarely possible for marketers to select either a low cost or differentiation strategy. Both must be pursued.

The real foundation for Porter's generic strategies are actually based in marketing and financial theory—to yield the highest profit, adopt strategies that keep sales at the highest possible level and costs at the lowest possible level. The question of the appropriate strategy is more complicated than deciding on one generic strategy to pursue. The people who should actually receive the credit for these generic strategies are Smith, for proposing the concept of differentiation, and Drucker, for introducing the marketing concept.

Most generic strategy typologies were created during a time when America was still the preeminent manufacturing power in the world. Today, with the rapid transformation toward service- and knowledge-based core competencies, the achievement of competitive advantage is no longer a simple matter of deciding in which of three or so strategic directions a firm should be headed. The purpose here is not to suggest that these generic strategy typologies be placed on the strategic planning history shelf, but simply to describe an alternative means of viewing their application in the strategy formulation process.

Strategic planning is as much as artform as a science. Multi-dimensional decisions are made that attempt to achieve a harmonious balance between the firm and its environment. As such, individuals with the broadest palette or widest array of beneficial theories and strategic options have the greatest potential to create successful strategies. The process is simply too diverse and even cryptic to be relegated to a "matching the round block to the round hole" procedure.

Generic strategies focus on parts of the strategic puzzle but do not offer a complete picture or package that can be utilized to determine he firm's most viable position in the market and, therefore, the business- and functional-level strategies it should pursue. Their essential value is that of reminding firms that the marketing concept (differentiation) and costs control are the central tasks of management.

Generic strategies are not normally included as a separate component of the strategic plan but are emphasized in each area to which they apply. For example, if the low-cost strategy was being used, concentration or product development strategies could include lowering the average cost of entrees with a high food cost. To allow for more price flexibility or profit, management or marketing strategies might focus on finding ways to decrease operating expenses and overhead. Financial accounting strategies could include regular meetings with the purchasing department to identify opportunities for reducing costs.

Of the following generic strategies, differentiation and low cost are generally considered the most important.

Differentiation

Differentiation can be defined as product identification and brand loyalty based on such unique features as superior product or service quality fast service, good location, recognizable name and associated image factors, a protected source of supply, and past advertising.

Essentially, this is any unique selling proposition (USP) that customers view as different from competitors and desirable, and that offers an advantage over competitors. The ideal differentiation strategy yields an SCA (sustainable competitive advantage) or at least a competitive advantage. The more difficult the advantage is to understand or replicate, the greater its benefit and the longer it can be used as a competitive weapon. Differentiation is a valuable strategy because it allows the firm to effectively position itself against competitors while at the same time gaining customer loyalty Customer loyalty may then allow the firm to decrease its advertising expenditures and, in many circumstances, increase its prices.

The strategy of offering an excellent-quality product will usually help a firm survive. The problem with this line of thinking is that there are many firms doing just that. But positive points of differentiation will help the firm become a solid competitor.

Matching a competitor is often relatively easy: observe its strategies and actions, then imitate them. Replicating critical points of differentiation may be considerably more difficult. If the point of differentiation consists of excellent locations, large sums of money and time will be required.

On the contrary, an exhibition kitchen would be somewhat easier. Imagination and research into customer wants and demand will help locate the most effective differentiation strategies. McDonald's has several major points of differentiation with its many convenient locations, recognizable sign, billions of dollars in past image-building advertising, and its reputation for consistency.

The Hyatt is known for quality services and large atriums. Subway Sandwich Shops are known for their fresh-baked bread and many locations. Houston's Restaurants are known for offering an upscale atmosphere with professional service and excellent food at casual dining prices. Because of each of these firms' size and financial strength, their points of differentiation are also sustainable competitive advantages.

One of the problems involved in the setting of grand strategies for the hospitality industry is that few strategies have the ability to develop into sustainable competitive advantages. Since there are relatively few firms with well-protected advantages, a business must realize that even though it should not stop looking for a major competitive advantage or points of differentiation, it will need to focus more on satisfying the customer with a quality product or service.

Kotler and Stonich propose that there are four stages of competitive marketing: making goods less costly; designing products to be different; making better products; and making and delivering goods and services faster than competitors (called turbo marketing). All four stages focus to a great degree on product differentiation-less costly, better, different, faster. (The making of less costly products in this instance is construed to be a form of product differentiation.)

To increase its competitive position, a firm must recognize and satisfy a market's demand for products and services in less time, that is, before competitors. A firm must also be able to reduce the time necessary for the delivery of those products or services.

As the importance of the target market's time becomes more apparent, all classes of hotels and restaurants are doing whatever they can to speed and simplify the delivery of food, beverages, and various services. For a lawyer or sales representative, waiting up to an hour for a table at an upscale restaurant represents lost billable hours or less time with clients.

Each business must analyze its target customer or peripheral markets to identify their wants for present and potential products and services. Kotler and Stonich theorize that as traditional sources of competitive advantage, low cost, and differentiation have been exploited, time compression or turbo marketing should be added to the next generation's list of generic strategies.

Low cost

Low cost means simply having an advantage in terms of any product costs and operating expense factors.

Examples are economies of scale from a large market share or relatively large purchases, inexpensive land or building, efficient operations, and cost minimization in such areas as advertising, sales, research and development, labor and supplies.

A low-cost generic strategy can have a multitude of benefits, such as helping to ride out a recession, being able to compete more aggressively through pricing strategies, absorbing increases in costs of goods, offering a lower price to customers, reducing the attractiveness of a new competitor entering the market, and overall financial flexibility. In essence, low-cost leadership provides the firm with the ability to be a more nimble competitor by increasing its financial options.

The typical low-cost leader has a large market share. This allows for larger purchases relative to competitors, which leads to economies of scale. Since this option is not available to every competitor, most firms must seek alternative means to gain cost advantages. Possibly the most important time to consider costs is when the business's concept is being planned.

At this time, decisions such as sites, building, equipment, product and service, and labor requirements are made that will have a major impact on costs for the life of the concept. If a restaurant concept were centered around a limited rather than an extensive menu, it might be possible to save money on the building (less space), equipment (fewer menu items), food costs (purchasing larger quantities of a smaller number of items), and labor costs (fewer cooks are generally required for smaller, simpler menus).

A major sandwich shop chain was established on a low-cost strategy. At one time it was one of the fastest-growing small chains in the country New owners decided that the decors should be upgraded—at a considerable expense. Sales did not improve, so 20% of the previously successful shops closed their doors because they could not absorb the higher overhead. In various recessions businesses can sign 20- to 30-year leases or purchase buildings that are frequently 20% less than prior market rates. Some firms have as their expansion strategy the takeover of businesses with these low-cost, long-term leases.

A low-cost strategy is imperative in the hospitality industry. This is because customers have a reasonable base of knowledge that allows them to compare each product or service with another. For example, it would be difficult for a casual restaurant to charge $14.95 for a chicken entree for which primary competitors are charging $9.95.

Customers know what chicken costs at the grocery and at other restaurants, so they will likely refuse to order it. Because of consumers' product knowledge and their ability to compare a product with other similar products, hospitality industry competitors must focus on having the lowest possible cost in their segment, which will allow them to offer a good value and show a reasonable profit.

In many other industries, when a company comes out with a new product or service that has previously not been available, the average customer may have nothing with which to compare its value. For example, a new computer component may cost little to produce but can be marked up several times more than related products. As competitors introduce alternatives, then price comparisons and customer knowledge will help force the price down.

Focus

The focus strategy means concentrating on one primary

product, a single or narrow market segment, or a limited geographic area. The core concept of the focus strategy is that the firm concentrates on a narrower strategic target and therefore is able to operate more effectively and efficiently than competitors with broader goals.

When a focus strategy is successful, the result is either low-cost leadership or high differentiation. For example, most upscale restaurants focus primarily on a single menu category, such as steaks or Italian or French cuisine, and a limited market segment, generally upper-middle- to upper-class. Market focus could include a geographic focus, as when a restaurant or hotel goes into locations that others do not want, or where there is not as much competition. The purpose of this and most focus strategies is to locate a protected niche that can be exploited and defended.

Preemptive

When a company is the first to bring its product or service to market or is first to introduce a unique strategy, it may achieve an advantage over future entrants or adopters. Domino's made the first major effort at offering pizza delivery Fuddrucker's was first with a made-from-scratch hamburger. Taco Cabana was first with a quality fast-food Mexican restaurant.

During the late 1980s, Taco Bell was the first major chain to focus on value. McDonald's was first with clean, inexpensive fast-food hamburgers. La Quinta was first with upgraded budget-priced hotel rooms for business travelers. The founders or leaders of each of these firms had highly developed inferential skills, The fact that they were first to offer their products helped position their companies as first in customers' minds when they needed their particular product or service. This fact, in many cases, fueled explosive growth that resulted in much higher than average P/E ratios.

When the average P/E ratio was around 15, several companies were over 50, some over 100. To put this perspective, the average privately owned restaurant is worth in the neighborhood of four to six times earnings, irrespective of assets. A growing chain of restaurants, also irrespective of assets, might be worth around 10 to 20 times assets. A fast-growing restaurant chain that is publicly traded and is utilizing a preemptive strategy could be worth between 50 and 100 times earnings. Hotel figures are less dramatic since expansion is generally less dramatic and the value of their real estate plays a much greater role in the assessment of their value.

One of the considerations when using a preemptive strategy is the number, size, and duration of the barriers that hinder competitors from duplicating one's own efforts. High-tech firms, because of patents and other proprietary technologies, have the greatest barrier-building assets.

Some manufacturing firms may gain control of raw materials or establish economies of scale in purchases, production, distribution, and so on. Service companies, because of their heavy reliance on labor and limited reliance on protected technologies, have fewer barriers available with which to defend their strategies. Since service industries find it difficult to protect a first-mover advantage, establishing a pattern of preemptive moves will help maintain the advantages of the strategy.

Synergy

When firms are considering any type of expansion, one of the key skills that must be available is that of synergy. Synergy, in the context of strategy, is already having some of the skills necessary for the new business. For example, if a business expands outside its current geographic markets, having good real estate people, trainers, and a corporate culture supportive of expansion would be synergistic generic strategies.

Product life cycle

The product life cycle (PLC) is an analysis of the actual or potential sales of a product or business segment through the various stages of its marketable life. It is also a means of mapping the strategic direction of the hotel or foodservice industry as a whole, by industry segments and concepts, or by the brand itself. The setting of effective strategies for the long term requires some knowledge of the general direction of similar businesses and the potential strategies that competitors will use. Although there cannot be a set rule as to what strategy a business should pursue, various circumstances within each state of the PLC tend to support a narrow range of options. The analysis can be used to ascertain the most reasonable strategic options for a business and can help to determine the potential strategies of competitors.

Introduction

The introductory phase for hospitality businesses is applicable only for new individual brands or for new concepts. The industry as a whole must be considered to be in the maturity stage because of its longevity Hospitality concepts considered as being in the introductory stage will generally be new types of business within market segments, such as gourmet delivery or a mini-room luxury-class hotel.

Occasionally, it will include a new segment, as when La Quinta Inns opened its first economy business-class hotel. For an individual business or brand, introduction is the highest-risk stage because the business is new and untested. It is also generally going up against competitors with loyal customers, a solid base of experience, and greater cash reserves.

Profits will usually be limited by high opening costs and normal inefficiencies caused by a lack of experience. Frequently, restaurants will open with limited cash and show an excellent profit from the start. In fact, many new restaurant concepts will have their best months during the introduction stage. This is caused by customers in the trade area anticipating the opening, then flocking to try the new establishment. Once this curiosity factor wears off, the restaurant will need to rely on its quality to keep sales up.

Since few customers may have heard of the business before, there will likely be a need for extensive use of promotional strategies. However, the ingenuity of the operator and other factors can limit the need for promotion of a new business.

The most common and frequently inherent problem with preopening and opening promotional campaigns is that a new business will generally have very little available cash for an effective campaign. This will force most businesses to rely heavily on product, pricing, and place (location and atmosphere) as their primary opening marketing strategies.

The need for promotion may be reduced with some type of pricing strategy, such as market penetration pricing-opening with a price lower than the competition with the purpose of attracting customers from competitors- or personal selling in the neighborhood. If the hotel or foodservice business has a good location (place strategy), much of the need for special promotions may be negated.

If the business is being opened as an extension of a well-known brand or, for hotels, if there is an effective reservation system in place at its introduction, such as for the Marriott's Residence Inns, then increased promotion may be limited to preopening selling. Afterward, the business could conceivably be on a firm footing from its opening day. If a product is unique in a way that creates an exceptional amount of word-of-mouth advertising, then promotion will not be as necessary.

Growth

If the business, concept, or segment survives the introduction stage, then there is normally a period of accelerated growth in sales. At this stage the product has been accepted by target customers as a suitable alternative to previous choices. This is generally the most profitable stage for any product category. When the business is new, mistakes are made that often limit profits and sales.

Experience will generally produce the most efficient employee schedules and the most effective product/service mix and promotional mix. Suppliers are more numerous and also in their own growth stage, so prices for food, beverage, and operating costs may be lower. Since profits are up, and it is evident that concept or segment will be growing for some time to come, competing firms will enter the market. Schlotzsky's Sandwich shops, based in Austin, Texas, was one of the original sandwich shops to bake bread fresh each day in the restaurants.

As the brand entered the growth stage, numerous competitors began employing similar concepts. If the leader can retain its position during this stage, surviving attacks from new entries and smaller followers, then, unless major mistakes are made, it will most likely retain its position. If a business can dominate a market through a penetration strategy, high entry costs, or a reputation for excellence, then competitors may think twice before entering. Houston's Restaurants of Atlanta, Georgia, have established a foothold in the casual upscale restaurant market, and though some competitors have surfaced, few are competing with them head on.

Maturity

Since the primary problems faced by most restaurants and hotels are saturated markets, declining profits, and price competition, as a group they can be said to be in the maturity phase of the product life cycle. At this stage sales are either increasing slightly or have leveled off.

Sales increases will be limited to natural market expansion, much as the growth of the population in the region or country, or when new occasions for use are developed. Individual brands, concepts, and segments may be at this or any stage in the PLC, but this is the current stage for the entire hotel and foodservice industries.

At maturity there are often too many competitors chasing the same customer. Each segment will see its share of closings as stronger concepts take business away from weaker competitors. Promotional strategies will be stressed, but quality and value will be the lasting competitive advantages.

Product differentiation will also come into play as people grow tired of the same offering and as societal trends and other environmental factors change. Entry or expansion for smaller competitors will come through the establishment of niches in the market. These will be either through a protected or as yet unexploited location, or through developing a differentiated product.

Tejas Cafes based in Conroe, Texas, have grown by opening restaurants in cities generally thought too small for major casual-dining competitors. The restaurant industry appears to move in a relatively consistent pattern from early to late maturity, then back to early maturity. As too many restaurants are opened, weaker businesses, for one reason or another, will not be able to compete and begin to close down. This is termed a shakeout and can happen for the entire industry or for a segment, concept, or brand.

Decline

Both the foodservice and hotel industries have experienced periods of decline. Foodservice establishments have quickly rebounded after dips in sales. However, hotels have not fared as well as the foodservice industry in recent years. Because of financial problems caused by overbuilding and overcapacity, the hotel industry during the late 1980s and early 1990s entered a period of decline. In the early and mid-1980s, money for expansion was easy to come by, so a large number of chains, franchisors, and independent operators were building at slightly inflated costs.

When the economy dipped, many operators in the overbuilt and heavily mortgaged industry were not able to survive, or they decided to keep the hotel as a real estate investment rather than for its value as a business. Even though the average hotel had been losing money for several years, each year it was losing less, and as of 1993, just over half of the industry was showing a profit. Things are expected to improve into the next century.

Like the restaurant industry, segments within the hotel industry are enjoying varying degrees of success. While the upscale and upper-midscale segments have been struggling, the midscale to lower-midscale and economy segments have been holding their own and in some areas showing moderate growth. The all-suites segment has fared the best but because of its higher rates is more vulnerable to a value-conscious consumer. During the late 1980s and early 1990s, the government-owned Resolution Trust Corporation (RTC) through hotel foreclosures became one of the largest hotel operators in the country. When restaurants experience major declines in revenues and negative bottom lines, closing the doors is a viable option. This is because there is little value to be gained, under the circumstances, from keeping a restaurant open. It will probably continue to lose money and could eventually lose much more than its salvage value. On the other hand, a hotel losing $15,000 per month, while not the best of circumstances, would pose a different problem than a restaurant with losses.

Since the hotel could have an asset value of several million dollars, owners are motivated to hold onto the property until a regular profit returns, or until a buyer is found. It is also more expensive to close a hotel than to keep it operating at minimal capacity. Once closed, carpeting, furniture, and paint tend to mildew, HVAC systems (heating, venting, and air conditioning) break down, 24-hour security is required, the property must be fenced in, vandalism becomes a problem, and so forth.

Some operators in the foodservice or hotel industries feel that because of the unique needs they serve-food and a place to sleep while traveling-they will probably never reach the end of the product life cycle. This is true to an extent. The hospitality industry as a whole will survive, but only those brands, concepts, or segments that modify their offerings to keep pace with consumer trends will be among the survivors.

Categories for the product life cycle

The PLC can be used to explain a product's potential for any relevant product category grouping, such as its industry, concepts, and primary product offering. Each product grouping analysis will yield a unique picture of a business's potential opportunities and threats. Since each category of the PLC encompasses many conceivable factors that may affect a business, there is no set position in any one PLC that would unquestionably indicate what strategy a business should pursue. Product categories for the product life cycle follow.

Industry

The broadest category is the industry. This product life cycle would show how the sales for all hotels or all foodservice establishments are progressing. The degree of effect on a particular business or brand will depend on many factors. If the industry PLC is growing at moderate pace, the company can generally assume that the economy and the majority of environmental factors are conducive to growth.

Industry segment

The industry segment would represent sales for a segment within the industry. There are several possible methods of segmenting the hotel and foodservice industries. The foodservice industry is commonly divided into fast-food, casual-dining, fine-dining, and institutional foodservice. Hotels segments could include economy, midscale, upper midscale and luxury.

Concepts

This would include types of businesses within each industry segment. Within the fast-food segment there are hamburgers, Mexican food, fried chicken, pizza, and Chinese food, among others. In the midscale hotel segment, typical classifications are downtown, airport, business, shopping, roadside/ highway, suites, inns, and resort.

Brand

This includes each different hotel or foodservice company, for example, Hilton hotels, Taco Bell restaurants, and ARAMARK Corporation for institutional foodservice.

Product or service offering

Each year unique products or services appear in restaurants and hotels. Many of these quickly perish as fads, while some will survive for varying lengths of time. Trends are new products or services, or variations of existing products and services, that have been accepted by various customer segments and widely adopted by business.

Paul Prudhomme's blackened style of cooking first appeared to be headed toward extinction—a fad. Few conceived that customers would want their fish, steak, or chicken essentially burnt. As the converts grew, the blackened style of cooking became a major trend. Other new products, such as butter sauces or California compilation sauces like blueberry vinaigrette for meats, can be considered as fads and have quickly faded. The ability to discover what new products or services customers will want is not easy. For some it is akin to using a crystal ball. Companies with well-developed marketing information systems, especially a thorough customer analysis, will have clues as to the next product or service customers will desire.

Generally, the safest approach, and one used by most operators, is to allow someone else to take the risk of introducing (pioneering) a new product (or service). If the product appears to be catching on, then being one of the first to offer it may be better than risking the fate of the pioneer. This strategy must, of course, be weighed against the sacrifice of not being the first to market a highly demanded product. Occasionally, there will be products that are obvious fads but, because of their current popularity, should be considered for the business.

Location

Each of the above categories can also be considered by their location. This could refer to country, region, state, county, city or part of a city For example, at the same time hotels may be suffering in one region, business could be booming in another.

Portfolio analysis

In portfolio analysis, a corporate-level strategy decision, individual businesses are viewed on the basis of such key performance factors or indicators as profit, market share, the competitive nature of industry, and the strengths and weaknesses of the business. Perhaps the most popular form of portfolio analysis has been the Boston Consulting Group (BCG) growth/share matrix. The primary purpose and contribution of the BCG matrix analysis is two-fold:

1. To provide a systematic means of integrating several businesses into a comprehensive corporate strategy. The analysis adds a measure of objectivity to the strategic selection process by quantifying a business's position.
2. To assign a purpose for each business unit. Under the BCG matrix each business is given a designation as one of the following:
   - (a) *Star*. Businesses with a high market share in a high-growth industry will normally be generating reasonable profits but, because of the necessity of financial investment for growth, may not be producing a positive cash flow. The business strategy will generally be for growth fueled by externally acquired capital.
   - (b) *Question marks*. businesses with a low relative market share in a high-growth industry will usually be in a growth phase, but with a weak financial position. This will normally necessitate investments from other

corporate business units. The business strategy for most question marks is usually for growth with funds being supplied from cash cows. If the business does not live up to expectations or if industry growth slows, then the question mark may become a dog.

(C) *Cash cows*. A business in a low-growth industry but with a high market share will often produce substantial profits and cash flow to be used for business units in other categories. The most frequent business strategy for a cash cow is to be milked for investment in stars or question marks. If there is little optimism for a stable future for the business, then the corporation might decide to pursue a harvest strategy of limiting maintenance investments.

(d) *Dogs*. Businesses with a low market share in a low-growth industry will vary between significant cash users to moderate cash generators. The business strategy for a dog is most often to divest, but occasionally to hold for possible strategic repositioning as a question mark or cash cow.

Though the BCG matrix was at one time at the forefront of corporate strategic planning theory, it is now studied primarily from a historical perspective and as a means of establishing a better understanding for more advanced methods of portfolio analysis. Among the key problems of the BCG matrix is that it focuses only on growth and market share.

Obviously, these two indicators are important, but much more is needed. For example, a restaurant could have a low market share with minimal industry growth but be producing an excellent profit. It also ignores many internal and environmental influences that will impact the business's future. For example, in a declining market, businesses will be closing down and be put up for sale, reducing supply and increasing the likelihood for improved demand for remaining competitors. This would also increase expansion opportunities through the acquisition of marginal performers.

Business strength

To solve some of the problems of the BCG growth/share matrix, a more thorough matrix analysis, the business strength/industry attractiveness matrix, was developed. The primary improvement of the business strength/industry attractiveness (BS/IA) matrix over the BCG matrix is that it allows for the analysis of multiple variables rather than only market share and growth.

The matrix is flexible in that it can be used to assess the performance of a single company or a group of companies under the same corporate umbrella, or as a tool to analyze the comparative strength of competitors.

Table 1

Business Strength/industry Attractiveness Values

Business Strength	*Weight (importance to firm; must add up to 10)*	*Rating (Performance; 1 = poor 10 = excellent)*	*Value (Weight × Rating)*
Profit	3	8	24
Product/service quality	3	8	24
Management skills	2	7	14
Locations	1	6	6
Atmosphere	1	5	5
Total value for business strength			73

Industry Attractiveness	Weight	Rating (Present trend; 1 = not attrac tive, 10 = very attractive	Value
Growth	2.5	5	12.5
Profit margins	3.5	7	24.5
Competitive intensity	3	5	15
Remote environment	1	7	7
Total value for industry attractiveness			59

Each of the key variables used must be given a weight, rating, and value. The process follows.

— The weight will be based on its importance to the company, relative to other selected variables. The total points must equal 10. If desired, decimals, such as 1.4, may be used. The weights can be based on their importance as determined by management or, when possible, by customer surveys. For example, financial performance would be weighted by management, whereas the weighting of operational performance factors could be determined by asking customers to complete a short survey that ranks the importance of selected factors.

— A rating (or grade) will be given for each business strength variable, designating the company's level of performance. For example, a strength would receive a high score, a weakness would receive a lower score. The ratings would be calculated on a ten-point basis as recommended for the category weight.

— The rating for each variable is then multiplied by its weight to obtain the variable's value.

— The values are individually summed for total value for business strength for that particular business.

— For industry attractiveness, influencing variables will be given a weight based on their importance to the business, and a rating based on favorable or unfavorable conditions in the environment relative to the variable. Primarily, does it indicate an opportunity or threat, now or in the future?

— The total value for industry attractiveness is calculated in the same manner as for business strength.

— The two scores for each business unit are then used to position the business on the matrix.

— As with the BCG matrix, the position on the matrix will indicate whether the overall business strategy for the individual firm should be to grow (invest in the business to expand it), hold (keep operating the business without liquidation of assets, invest only enough capital to remain competitive), harvest (keep operating the business but do not invest beyond that necessary to stay in business), or divest.

Neither the BCG matrix nor the BS/IA matrix will provide all the answers to corporate-level business strategy decisions. Each business and its competitors must be analyzed in depth to make the most accurate strategic choice possible. The matrix analysis at least adds some consistency to the process. An additional use for matrix analysis is to construct a competitor's portfolio matrix to forecast what potential strategies might be selected. It can also be utilized as a more sophisticate form of a competitor's perceptual map.

Strategies for different industry positions

There are hundreds of thousands of hospitality firms, each with varying amounts of resources and abilities and different objectives. Each business will decide, based on its position in the industry, what strategies are possible and logical for it to pursue. While there is no set strategy that every business of a particular type, size, or financial strength should follow, there are historical parameters of engagement that can be utilized to increase the possibility of success. Much of what is practiced in marketing strategies comes from military terminology. Flanking attacks, guerrilla attacks, counter-offensives, encirclement attacks, and many other strategies are not unique to marketing, but originated and were perfected in the ultimate struggle—war—where lives and countries were at stake. Various marketing and strategic business writers have different terms for a business's position in its industry. The categorization selected for this book is that of the market leaders, market challengers, and market nichers.

The leader

Each segment within the hotel and foodservice industries will have a leader. For the hospitality industry, the primary measure of leadership is overall sales, plus unit sales for restaurants and REVPAR for hotels (average daily rate times occupancy percentage). Sometimes this is a clear and well-recognized leader, such as McDonald's in the fast-food sector.

For some segments, the lead position may not be as easily recognized as in the case of upper-midscale hotels, with the Hilton, Marriott, and Hyatt. Unlike in many industries, where certain leaders capture enough of the market to deter most competitors, costs of entry are exorbitant, and economies of scale rule, leaders in the hospitality business must compete head-on with rivals on a near-even footing. The greater a firm's reliance on people rather than equipment, the fewer advantages there are for the leader of that industry. There is no room in the lightbulb industry for 10,000 competitors to attack General Electric, but there are well over 600,000 foodservice establishments vying for the customer's food dollar.

Leaders in the hospitality industry will benefit from name recognition and financial resources that allow for larger ad budgets and faster expansion, but each leader's primary focus will be on competing with rivals in its trade area. It is often more important for hotels to face competition within each market rather than on a national basis.

National campaigns will always be important in gaining customers for their initial visit, but individual business units of the chain will have the responsibility of keeping them. A Marriott across the street from a Crowne Plaza (Holiday Inn) enjoys a name recognition benefit, but not much else. Each hotel will have to compete based on its relative individual merits rather that fact that one is an industry leader and one is a challenger. Even McDonald's, the Goliath of the fast-food industry, must address each trade area challenger as a potentially worthy opponent.

For leaders to remain on top, they must focus on protecting their strengths, essentially the continuation of what got them to their present position. They must also incorporate strategies that will make it more difficult for challengers to gain momentum. This could be through increasing market penetration, product additions, or diversifying into related businesses (concentric diversification).

A common problem for market leaders is that they focus so much on their strengths that they miss major shifts in their competitive environment. A more and more frequent strategy of market leaders is that of a commitment to core strategies, plus the adoption of successful strategies of market challengers and nichers.

Holiday Inn has imitated several of its largest challengers by adding five different classes of hotels to its portfolio.

Also, unlike in most industries, a leadership role or high market share does not equate with profit or growth. McDonald's is the leader in fast food and it does show a good profit, but that profit is from running an efficient operation. Burger King, Hardee's, and the Marriott, at various times, found that being a major player carries few benefits. The lesson learned is that the results of strategic actions are essentially proportionate to the size of the company. A small company selecting the wrong strategy may lose $20,000, perhaps a major percentage of their cash reserves.

Challengers and market nichers

Most firms within an industry segment will utilize very similar strategies, regardless of their position. When this happens, the results are generally that the business with the largest market share will win. The leader has more experience, money, penetration, recognition, and customer loyalty, so it can easily defeat an opponent that plays by their rules. Imitating the leader may allow a business to survive, but in today's competitive environment trying to survive may lead to demise.

For long-term success, every business must gain some type of an advantage. If a challenger or nicher is to increase its share of the market, it must change the rules of the game with the goal of neutralizing or temporarily paralyzing the leader or significant competitor. Large corporations have set ways of doing things, and after all, they are the leaders, so it has worked for them. They also generally have rigid organizational structures that make a rapid response difficult. While the leader is stunned, or sitting back thinking that things will soon be back to normal, the challenger can make significant gains.

There are various types of attacks for the challenger or nicher. One is a flanking attack to circumvent the strengths of the leader. Pizza Hut and Pizza Inn thought little of Dominos' strategy of delivery until their market shares were severely eroded. La Quinta Inns developed a strategy based on the theory that business and pleasure travelers would accept fewer services in return for lower rates. Choice Hotels International, composed of Sleep, Comfort, Quality Clarion, Econolodge, and Roadway, among others, decided to set up an advanced reservation system, then assemble a menu of hotels so they could offer each caller a hotel room within their price range.

The safest strategy for the nicher is to find a geographic niche that leaders or challengers are not likely to pursue. For a restaurant, this could provide years of relative protection from major competition. While hotels can still find geographic niches, because of the much larger investment and broader customer base, they must be certain that the location is worth the risk.

6

Staffing for Housekeeping Operations

The development of the Area Responsibility Plan and the House Breakout Plan before opening led to preparation of the Department Staffing Guide, which will be a major tool in determining the need for employees in various categories. The housekeeping manager and laundry manager should now be on board and assisting in the development of various job descriptions.

The hotel human resources department would also have been preparing for the hiring event. They would have advertised a mass hiring for all categories of personnel to begin on a certain date about two weeks before opening. Even though this chapter reflects a continuation of the executive housekeeper's planning for opening operations, the techniques described apply to any ongoing operation, except that the magnitude of selection, orientation, and training activities will not be as intense. Also, the fourth activity--development of existing employees-is normally missing in opening operations but is highly visible in ongoing operations.

Employee requisition

Once job specifications have been developed for every position, employee requisitions are prepared for first hirings (and for any follow-up needs for the human resources department).The designation as to whether the requisition is for a new or a replacement position and the number of employees required for a specific requisition number. The human resources department will advertise, take applications, and screen to fill each requisition by number until all positions are filled. For example, the first requisition for GRAs may be for 20 GRAs. The human resources department will continue to advertise for, take applications, and screen employees for the housekeeping department and will provide candidates for interview by department managers until 20 GRAs are hired. Should any be hired and require replacing, a new employee requisition will be required.

Staffing housekeeping positions

There are several activities involved in staffing a housekeeping operation. Executive housekeepers must select and interview employees, participate in an orientation program, train newly hired employees, and develop employees for future growth. Each of these activities will now be discussed.

Selecting employees

Each area of the United States has its own demographic situations that affect the availability of suitable employees for involvement in housekeeping or environmental service operations. For example, in one area an exceptionally high response rate from people seeking food service work may occur and a low response rate from people seeking housekeeping positions may occur. In another area the reverse may be true, and people interested in housekeeping work may far outnumber those interested in food service.

Surveys among hotels or hospitals in your area will indicate the best source for various classifications of employees. Advertising campaigns that will reach these employees are the best method of locating suitable people. Major classified ads associated with mass hirings will specify the need for food service personnel, front desk clerks, waiters, waitresses, housekeeping personnel, and maintenance people. Such ads may yield surprising results. If the volume of response for housekeeping personnel is insufficient to provide a suitable hiring base, the following sources may be investigated:

1. Local employment agencies
2. Flyers posted on community bulletin boards
3. Local church organizations
4. Neighbourhood canvass for friends of recently hired employees
5. Direct radio appeals to local home makers
6. Organizations for underprivileged ethnic minorities, and mentally disabled people. (It should be noted that many mentally disabled persons are completely capable of performing simple housekeeping tasks and are dependable and responsible people seeking an opportunity to perform in a productive capacity.)

If these sources do not produce the volume of applicants necessary to develop a staff, it may become necessary to search for employees in distant areas and to provide regular transportation for them to and from work. If aliens are hired, the department manager must take great care to ensure that they are legal residents of this country and that their green cards are valid.

More than one hotel department manager has had an entire staff swept away by the Department of Immigration after hiring people who were illegal aliens. Such unfortunate action has required the immediate assistance of all available employees (including management) to fill in.

Whether you are involved in a mass hiring or in the recruiting of a single employee, a systematic and courteous procedure for processing applicants is essential.

For example, in the opening of the Los Angeles Airport Marriott, 11,000 applicants were processed to fill approximately 850 positions in a period of about two weeks. The magnitude of such an operation required a near assembly-line technique, but a personable and positive experience for the applicants still had to be maintained.

The efficient handling of lines of employees, courteous attendance, personal concern for employee desires, and reference to suitable departments for those unfamiliar with what the hotel or hospital has to offer all become earmarks for how the company will treat its employees. The key to proper handling of applicants is the use of a control system whereby employees are conducted through the steps of application, prescreening, and if qualified, reference to a department for interview.

Note the opportunity for employees to express their desires for a specific type of employment. Even though an employee may desire involvement in one classification of work, he or she may be hired for employment in a different department. Also, employees might not be aware of the possibilities available in a particular department at the time of application or may be unable to locate in desired departments at the time of mass hirings.

Employees who perform well should therefore be given the opportunity to transfer to other departments when the opportunities arise. According to laws regulated by federal and state Fair Employment Practices Agencies (FEPA), no person may be denied the opportunity to submit application for employment for a position of his or her choosing. Not only is the law strict on this point, but companies in any way benefiting from interstate commerce (such as hotels and hospitals) may not discriminate in the hiring of people based on race, colour, natural origin, or religious preference. Although specific hours and days of the week may be specified, it is a generally accepted fact that hotels and hospitals must maintain personnel operations that provide the opportunity for people to submit applications without prejudice.

Prescreening applicants

The prescreening interview is a staff function normally provided to all hotel or hospital departments *human resources* section of the organization. Prescreening is a preliminary interview process in unqualified applicants-those applicants who do not meet the criteria for a job as specified in the job specification-special qualifications-are selected (or screened) out. For example, an applicant for a secretarial job that requires the incumbent to take shorthand and be able to type 60 words a minute may be screened out if the applicant is not able to pass a relevant typing and shorthand test. The results of prescreening are usually coded for internal use and are indicated on the Applicant Processing Record.

If a candidate is screened out by the personnel section, he or she should be told the reason immediately and be thanked for applying for employment. Applicants who are not screened out should either be referred to a specific department for interview or, if all immediate positions are filled, have their applications placed in a department pending file for future reference. All applicants should be told that hiring decisions will be made by individual department managers based on the best qualifications from among those interviewed.

A suggested agenda for a prescreening interview is as follows:

1. The initial contact should be cordial and helpful. Many employees are lost at this stage because of inefficient systems established for handling applicants.

2. During the prescreening interview, try to determine what the employee is seeking, whether such a position is available, or, if not, when such a position might become available.
3. Review the work history as stated on the application to determine whether the applicant meets the obvious physical and mental qualifications, as well as important human qualifications such as emotional stability, personality, honesty, integrity, and reliability.
4. Do not waste time if the applicant is obviously not qualified or if no immediate position is available. When potential vacancies or a backlog of applicants exists, inform the candidate. Be efficient in stating this to the applicant. Always make sure that the applicant gives you a phone number in order that he or she may be called at some future date. Because most applicants seeking employment are actively seeking immediate work, applications over 30 days old are usually worthless.
5. If at all possible, an immediate interview by the department manager should be held after screening. If this is not possible, a definite appointment should be made for the candidate's interview as soon as possible.

The interview

Interviews should be conducted by a manager of the department to which the applicant has been referred, In ongoing operations, it is often wise to also allow the supervisor for whom the new employee will work to visit with the candidate in order that the supervisor may gain a feel for how it would be to work together, The supervisor's view should be considered, since a harmonious relationship at the working level is important. Although the acceptance of an employee remains a prerogative of management, it would be unwise to accept an employee into a position when the supervisor has reservations about the applicant.

Certain personal characteristics should be explored when interviewing an employee. Some of these characteristics are native skills, stability, reliability, experience, attitude toward employment, personality, physical traits, stamina, age, sex, education, previous training, initiative, alertness, appearance, and personal cleanliness. Although employers may not discriminate against race, sex, age, religion, and nationality, overall considerations may involve the capability to lift heavy objects, enter men's or women's restrooms, and so on.

In a housekeeping (or environmental services) department, people should be employed who find enjoyment in housework at home. Remember that character and personality cannot be completely judged from a person's appearance. Also, it should be expected that a person's appearance will never be better than when that person is applying for a job.

Letters of recommendation and references should be carefully considered. Seldom will a letter of recommendation be adverse, whereas a telephone call might be most revealing. If it were necessary to select the most important step in the selection process, interviewing would be it. Interviewing is the step that separates those who will be employed from those who will not. Poor interviewing techniques can make the process more difficult and may produce a result that can be both frustrating and damaging for both parties.

In addition, inadequate interviewing will result in gaining incorrect information, being confused about what has been said, suppression of information, and, in some circumstances, complete withdrawal from the process by the candidate.

The following is a well-accepted list of the steps for a successful interview process.

1. *Be prepared.* Have a checklist of significant questions ready to ask the candidate. Such questions may be prepared from the body of the job description. This preparation will allow the inter viewer to assume the initiative in the interview
2. *Find a proper place to conduct the interview* The applicant should be made to feel comfortable. The interview should be conducted in a quiet, relaxing atmosphere where there is privacy that will bring about a confidential conversation.
3. *Practice.* People who conduct interviews should practice interviewing skills periodically. Several managers may get together and discuss inter viewing techniques that are to be used.
4. *Be tactful and courteous.* Put the applicant at ease, but also control the discussions and lead to important questions.
5. *Be knowledgeable.* Be thoroughly familiar with the position for which the applicant is interviewing in order that all of the applicant's questions may be answered. Also, have a significant back ground knowledge in order that general information about thc company may be given.
6. *Listen.* Encourage the applicant to talk. This may be done by asking questions that are not prone to be answered by a yes or no. If people are comfortable and are asked questions about themselves, they will usually speak freely and give information that specific questions will not always bring out. Applicants will usually talk if there is a feeling that they are not being misunderstood.
7. *Observe.* Much can be learned about an applicant just by observing reactions to questions, attitudes about

work, and, specifically, attitudes about providing service to others. Observation is a vital step in the interviewing process.

Interview pitfills

Perhaps of equal importance to the interviewing technique are the following pitfalls, which should be avoided while interviewing.

1. Having a feeling that the employee will be just right based on a few outstanding characteristics rather than on the sum of all characteristics noted.
2. Being influenced by neatness, grooming, expensive clothes, and an extroverted personality—none of which has much to do with housekeeping competency
3. Overgeneralizing, whereby interviewers assume too much from a single remark (for instance, an applicant's assurance that he or she "really wants to work").
4. Hiring the boomer, that is, the person who always wants to work in a new property; unfortunately, this type of person changes jobs whenever a new property opens.
5. Projecting your own background and social status into the job requirement. Which school the applicant attended or whether the applicant has the "proper look" is beside the point. It is job performance that is going to count.
6. Confusing strengths with weaknesses and vice versa. What is construed by one person to be over-aggressiveness might be interpreted by another as confidence, ambition, and potential for leadership, the last two traits being in chronic short supply in most housekeeping departments. These are the very characteristics that make it possible for management

to promote from within and develop new supervisors and managers.

7. Being impressed by a smooth talker-or the reverse: assuming that silence reflects strength and wisdom. The interviewer should concentrate on what the applicant is saying rather than on how it is being said. Then decide whether his or her personality will fit into the organization.
8. Being tempted by over-qualified applicants. People with experience and education that far exceed the job requirements may be unable for some reason to get a job commensurate with their background. Even if such applicants are not concealing skeletons in the closet, they still tend to become frustrated and dissatisfied with jobs far below their level of abilities.

The application of the techniques and avoidance of the pitfalls will be valuable tools in the selection of competent personnel for the housekeeping and environmental service departments.

For many years, the approach of many managers was to write a job description and then fill it by attempting to find the perfect person. This approach may overlook many qualified people, such as disadvantaged people or slow learners. Job descriptions may be analysed in two ways when filling positions: (1) what is actually required to do the work, and (2) what is desirable. Is the ability to read or write really necessary for the job? Is the ability to learn quickly really necessary? A person who does not read or write or who is a slow learner can be trained and will make an excellent employee.

True, it may take additional time, but the reward will be a loyal employee as well as less turnover. It has been proven many times that those who are disadvantaged or slightly retarded, once trained, will perform consistently well for longer periods. There are agencies who seek out companies that will try to hire such people.

Results of the interview

If the results of an interview are negative and rejection is indicated, the candidate should be informed as soon as possible. A pleasant statement, such as "others interviewed appear to be more qualified," is usually sufficient. This information can be handled in a straightforward and courteous manner and in such a way that the candidate will appreciate the time that has been taken during the interview. When the results of the interview are positive, a statement indicating a favourable impression is most encouraging. However, no commitment should be made until a *reference check* has been conducted.

Reference checks

In many cases, reference checks are made only to verify that what has been said in the application and interview is in fact true. Many times applicants are reluctant to explain in detail why previous employment situations have come to an end. It is more important to hear the actual truth about a prior termination from the application than it is to hear that they simply have been terminated. Reference checks, in order of desirability, are as follows:

1. Personal (face-to-face) meetings are the least available but provide the most accurate information when they can be arranged.
2. Telephone discussions are the next best and most often used approach. For critical positions, an in-depth conversation by telephone between the potential new manager and the prior manager is most desirable; otherwise a simple verification of data is sufficient to ensure honesty.

3. The least desirable reference is the written recommendation, since managers are extremely reluctant to state a frank and honest opinion that may be later used against them in court.

Applicants who are rated successful at an interview should be told that a check of their references will be conducted, and, pending favourable responses, they will be contacted by the personnel department within two days. Applicants who are currently employed will normally ask that their current employer not be contacted for a reference check. This request should be honoured at all times. Applicants who are currently working will usually want to give proper notice to their current employer. If the applicant chooses not to give notice, chances are no notice will be given at the time he or she leaves your hotel. In some cases, the applicant gives notice and upon doing so is "cut loose" immediately. If such is the case, the applicant should be told to contact the department manager immediately in order that the employee may be put to work as soon as possible.

Interview skills versus turnover

There is no perfect interviewer, interviewee, or resultant hiring or rejection decision of an applicant. We can only hope to improve our interviewing skills in order that the greatest degree of success in employee retention can be obtained. The executive housekeeper should expect that 25 percent of initial hires into a housekeeping department will not be employed for more than three months. (This is primarily because the housekeeping skills are easily learned and the position is paid at or near minimum wage.) Some new housekeeping departments have as much as a 75 percent turnover rate in the first three months of operation.

Certainly this figure can be improved upon with adequate attention to the interviewing and selection processes. However, regardless of the outcome of the interview, the processing record should be properly endorsed and returned to the personnel department for processing.

Orientation

A carefully planned, concerned, and informational orientation program is significant to the first impressions that a new employee will have about the hospital or hotel in general and the housekeeping department in particular. Too often, a new employee is told where the work area and restroom are, given a cursory explanation of the job, then put to work. It is not uncommon to find managers putting employees to work who have not even been processed into the organization, an unfortunate situation that usually is discovered on payday when there is no paycheck for the new employee. Such blatant disregard for the concerns of the employee can only lead to poor reception of the company.

A planned orientation program will eliminate this type of activity and will bring the employee into the company with personal concern and with a greater possibility for a successful relationship. Every good orientation program is usually made up of four phases: employee acquisition, receipt of an employee's handbook, tour of the facility, and an orientation meeting.

Employee acquisition

Once a person is accepted for employment, the applicant is told to report for work at a given time and place, and that place should be the personnel department. Preemployment procedures Could take as much as one-half day, and department managers eager to start new employees to work should allow time for a proper employee acquisition into the organization. At this time it should be ensured that the application is complete and any additional information pertaining to employment history that may be necessary to obtain the necessary work permits and credentials is on hand.

Usually the security department will record the entry of a new employee into the staff and will provide instructions regarding use of employee entrances, removing parcels from the premises, and employee parking areas. Application for work permits, and drug testing, will be scheduled where applicable. All documents required by the hotel's health and welfare insurer should be completed, and instructions should be given about immediately reporting accidents, no matter how slight, to supervisors. The federal government requires that every employer submit a W-4 (withholding statement) for each employee on the payroll.

The employee must complete this document and give it to the company. Mandatory deductions from pay should be explained (federal and state income tax and Social Security FICA), as should other deductions that may be required or desired. At this time, some form of personal action document is usually initiated on the new employee and is placed in the employee's permanent record.

The Personnel Action Form (PAF) is serially numbered, is created from data stored on magnetic discs, and is maintained in the employee's personnel file. When a change has to be made, such as job title, marital status, or rate of pay, the PAF is retrieved from the employee's record, changes are made under the item to be changed, and the corrected PAF is used to change the data in the computer storage. Once new information is stored, a new PAF is created and placed in the employee's record to await the next need for processing. A longtime employee might have many PAFs stored in the personnel file. When either regular or special performance appraisals are given, the last (most current) PAF will be used to record the appraisal.A standard form used to record such appraisals, as well as written warnings and matters involving terminations. These forms are Usually found on the reverse side of the PAR Since performance appraisals may signify a raise in pay, the appropriate pay increase information would be indicated on the front side of the PAIR.

All recordings on PAR, whether on one side or both, require the submission of data, storage of information, and creation of a new PAF to be stored in the employee's record. The PAF and performance appraisal system should be thoroughly explained to the new employee, along with assignment of a payroll number. The employer should also explain how and when the staff is paid and when the first paycheck may be expected.

The employee handbook

The new employee should be provided with a copy of the Hotel or Hospital Employee's Handbook and should be told to read it thoroughly. Since the new housekeeping employee is not working just for the housekeeping department but is to become integrated as a member of the entire staff, reading this handbook is extremely important to ensure that proper instructions In the rules and regulations of the hotel are presented. The handbook should be developed in such a way as to inspire the new employee to become a fully participating member of the organization.

Familiarization tour of the facilities

Upon completion of the acquisition phase, a facility tour should be conducted for one or all new employees. For new facilities, access to the property should be gained within about one week before opening, and many new employees can be taken on a tour simultaneously. It is possible for employees to work in the hotel housekeeping department for years and have visited the showroom, dining rooms, ballrooms, or even the executive office areas. A tour of the complete facility melds employees into the total organization, and a complete informative tour should never be neglected. For ongoing operations, after acquisition the new employee may be turned over to a department supervisor, who becomes the tour director. An appreciation of the total involvement of each employee is strengthened when a facilities tour is complete and thorough. If necessary, the property tour might be postponed until after the orientation meeting; however, the orientation activity of staffing is not complete until a property tour is conducted.

Orientation meeting

Orientation meetings should not be conducted until the employee has had an opportunity to become at least partially familiar with the surroundings. After approximately two weeks, the employee will have many questions about experiences, the new job, training, and the rules and regulations listed in the Property and Department handbooks (see section on training).

Employee orientation meetings that are scheduled too soon fail to answer many questions that will develop within the first two weeks of employment. The meeting should be held in a comfortable setting with refreshments provided. It is usually conducted by the director of human resources and is attended by as many of the facility managers as possible. Most certainly, the general manager or hospital administration members of the executive committee, the security director, and the new employees department head should attend. Each of these managers should have an opportunity to welcome the new employees and give them a chance to associate names with faces.

All managers and new employees should wear name tags. In orientation meetings, a brief history of the company and company goals should be presented. A planned orientation meeting should not be concluded without someone stressing the importance of each position. Every position must have a purpose behind it and is therefore important to the overall functioning of the facility. The orientation meeting should be scheduled to allow for many questions. And there should be someone in attendance who can answer all of them.

Although the new employee will be gaining confidence and security in the position as training ends and work is actually performed, informal orientation may continue for quite some time. The formal orientation, however, ends with the orientation meeting (although the facility tour may be conducted after the meeting). Finally, it should be remembered that good orientation procedures lead to worker satisfaction and help quiet the anxieties and fears that a new employee may have. When a good orientation is neglected, the seeds of dissatisfaction are planted.

Training

The efficiency and economy by which any department will operate will depend on the ability of each member of the organization to do his or her job. Such ability will depend in part on past experiences, but more commonly it can be credited to the type and quality of training offered. Employees, regardless of past experiences, always need some degree of training before starting a new job.

Small institutions may try to avoid training by hiring people who are already trained in the general functions with which they will be involved. However, most institutions recognize the need for training that is specifically oriented toward the new experience and will have a documented training program. Some employers of housekeeping personnel find it easier to train completely unskilled and untrained personnel. In such cases, bad or undesirable practices do not have to be trained out of an employee.

Previous experience and education should, however, be analysed and considered in the training of each new employee in order that efficiencies in training can be recognized. If an understanding of department standards and policies can be demonstrated by a new employee, that portion of training may be shortened or modified. However, skill and ability must be demonstrated before training can be altered. Finally, training is the best method to communicate the company's way of doing things, without which the new employee may do work contrary to company policy.

First training

First training of a new employee actually starts with a continuation of *department* orientation. When a new employee is turned over to the housekeeping or environmental services department, orientation usually continues by familiarizing the employee with *department rules and regulations.* Many housekeeping departments have their own Department Employee Handbooks.

Training may be defined as those activities that are designed to help an employee begin performing tasks for which he or she is hired or to help the employee improve performance in a job already assigned. The purpose of training is to enable an employee to begin an assigned job or to improve upon techniques already in use. In hotel or hospital housekeeping operations, there are three basic areas in which training activity should take place: skills, attitudes, and knowledge.

Skills training. A sample list of skills in which a basic housekeeping employee must be trained follows:

1. *Bed making:* Specific techniques; company policy
2. *Vacuuming.* Techniques; use and care of equipment
3. *Dusting:* Techniques; Use of products
4. *Window and mirror cleaning:* Techniques and products
5. *Setup awareness.-* Room setups; what a properly serviced room should look like
6. *Bathroom cleaning:* Tub and toilet sanitation; appearance; methods of cleaning and results desired
7. *Daily routine:* An orderly procedure for the conduct of the day's work; daily communications
8. *Caring for and using equipment:* Housekeeper cart; loading
9. *Industrial safety:* Product use; guest safety; fire; and other emergencies

The best reference for the skills that require training is the job description for which the person is being trained.

Employees need guidance in their attitudes about tile work that must be done. They need to be guided in their thinking about rooms that may present a unique problem in cleaning. Attitudes among section housekeepers need to be such that, occasionally, when rooms require extra effort to be brought back to standard, it is viewed as being a part of rendering service to the guest who paid to enjoy the room. Carol Mondesir, director of housekeeping, Sheraton Centre, Toronto states that

> A hotel is meant to be enjoyed and, occasionally, the rooms are left quite messed up. However, as long as they're not vandalized, it's part of the territory. The whole idea of being in the hospitality business is to make the guest's stay as pleasant as possible. The rooms are there to be enjoyed.

Positive relationships with various agencies and people also need to be developed.

Below is a list of areas in which attitude guidance is important.

1. The guest/patient
2. The department manager and immediate supervisor
3. A guestroom that is in a state of great disarray
4. The hotel and company
5. The uniform
6. Appearance
7. Personal hygiene

The most important task of the trainer is to prepare new employees to meet standards. With this aim in mind, sequence of performance in cleaning a guestroom is most important in order that efficiency in accomplishing day-to-day tasks may be developed. In addition, the *best method* of accomplishing a task should be presented to the new trainee. Once the task has been learned, the next thing is to meet standards, which may not necessarily mean doing the job the way the person has been trained.

Areas of knowledge in which the employee needs to be trained are as follows:

1. Thorough knowledge of the hotel layout; employee must be able to give directions and to tell the guest about the hotel, restaurants, and other facilities
2. Knowledge of employee rights and benefits
3. Understanding of grievance procedure
4. Knowing top managers by sight and by name

Ongoing training

There is a need to conduct ongoing training for all employees, regardless of how long they have been members of the department. There are two instances when additional training is needed: (1) the purchase of new equipment and (2) change in or unusual employee behaviour while on the job. When new equipment is purchased, employees need to know how the new equipment differs from present equipment, what new skills or knowledge are required to operate the equipment, who will need this knowledge, and when. New equipment may also require new attitudes about work habits.

Employee behaviour while on the job that is seen as an indicator for additional training may be divided into two categories: events that the manager witnesses and events that the manager is told about by the employees. Events that the manager witnesses that indicate a need for training are frequent employee absence, considerable spoilage of products, carelessness, a high rate of accidents, and resisting direction by supervisors.

Events that the manager might be told about that indicate a need for training are that something doesn't work right (product isn't any good), something is dangerous to work with, something is making work harder.

Although training is vital for any organization to function at top efficiency, it is expensive. The money and man-hours expended must therefore be worth the investment. There must be a balance between the dollars spent training employees and the benefits of productivity and high-efficiency performance.

A simple method of determining the need for training is to measure performance of workers: Find out what is going on at present on the job, and match this performance with what should be happening. The difference, if any, describes how much training is needed. In conducting performance analysis, the following question should be asked: Could the employee do the job or task if his or her life depended on the result? If the employee *could not* do the job even if his or her life depended on the outcome, there is a deficiency of knowledge (DK). If the employee could have done the job if his or her life depended on the outcome, but did not, there is a deficiency of execution (DE).

Some of the causes of deficiencies of execution include task interference, lack of feedback (employee doesn't know when the job is being performed correctly or incorrectly), and the balance of consequences (some employees like doing certain tasks better than others). If either deficiency of knowledge or deficiency of execution exists, training must be conducted. The approach or the method of training may differ, however. Deficiencies of knowledge can be corrected by training the employee to do the job, then observing, correcting as necessary until the task is proficiently performed. Deficiency of execution is usually corrected by searching for the underlying cause of lack of performance, not by teaching the actual task.

Training methods

There are numerous methods or ways to conduct training. Each method has its own advantages and disadvantages, which must be weighed in the light of benefits to be gained. Some methods are more expensive than others but are also more effective in terms of time required for comprehension and proficiency that must be developed. Several useful methods of training housekeeping personnel are listed and discussed.

Using on-the-job training (OJT), a technique in which "learning by doing" is the advantage, the instructor demonstrates the procedure and then watches the students perform it. With this technique, one instructor can handle several students. In housekeeping operations, the instructor is usually a GRA who is doing the instructing in the rooms that have been assigned for cleaning that day. The OJT method is not operationally productive until the student is proficient enough in the training tasks to absorb part of the operational load.

With simulation training, a model room (unrented) is set up and used to train several employees. Whereas OJT requires progress toward daily production of ready rooms, simulation requires that the model room not be rented. In addition, the trainer is not productive in cleaning ready rooms. The advantages of simulation training are that it allows the training process to be stopped, discussed, and repeated if necessary~ Simulation is an excellent method provided the trainer's time is paid for out of training funds and clean room production is not necessary during the workday.

The coach-pupil method is similar to OJT except that each instructor has only one student (a one-to-one relationship). This method is desired provided that there are enough qualified instructors to have several training units in progress at the same time.

The lecture method reaches the largest number of students per instructor. Practically all training programs use this type of instruction for certain segments. Unfortunately, the lecture method can be the dullest training technique and therefore requires instructors who are gifted in presentation capabilities. In addition ' space for lectures may be difficult to obtain and may require special facilities.

The conference method of instruction is often referred to as workshop training. This technique involves a group of students who formulate ideas, do problem solving, and report on projects. The conference or workshop technique is excellent for supervisory training.

When new products or equipment are being introduced, demonstrations are excellent. Many demonstrations may be conducted by vendors and purveyors as a part of the sale of equipment and products. Difficulties may arise when language barriers exist. It is also important that no more information be presented than can be absorbed in a reasonable period of time; otherwise misunderstandings may arise.

Training aids

Many hotels will use training aids in a conference room or will post messages on an employee bulletin board. Aside from the usual training aids such as chalkboards, bulletin boards, charts, graphs, and diagrams, photographs can supply clear and accurate references for how rooms should be set up, maids' carts loaded, and routines accomplished. Most housekeeping operations will have films on guest contact and courtesy that may also be used in training. Motion pictures speak directly to many people who may not understand proper procedures from reading about them. Many training techniques may be combined to develop a well-rounded training plan.

Development

It is possible to have two students sitting side by side in a classroom, with one being trained and the other being developed. Recall that the definition of training is preparing a person to do a job for which he or she is hired or to improve upon performance of a current job. Development is preparing a person for advancement or to assume greater responsibility. The techniques are the same, but the end result is quite different.

Whereas training begins after orientation of an employee who is hired to do a specific job, upon introduction of new equipment, or upon observation and communication with employees indicating a need for training, development begins with the identification of a specific employee who has shown potential for advancement. Training for promotion or to improve potential is in fact development and must always include a much neglected type of training-supervisory training.

Many forms of developmental training may be given on the property; other forms might include sending candidates to schools and seminars. Developmental training is associated primarily with supervisors and managerial development and may encompass many types of experiences.

Development of individuals within the organization looks to future potential and promotion of employees. Specifically, those employees who demonstrate leadership potential should be developed through supervisory training for advancement to positions of greater, responsibility. Unfortunately, many outstanding workers have their performance rewarded by promotion but are given no development training. The excellent section housekeeper who is advanced to the position of senior housekeeper without the benefit of supervisory training is quickly seen to be unhappy and frustrated and may possibly become a loss to the department. It is therefore most essential that individual potential be developed in an orderly and systematic manner, or else this potential may never be recognized.

While undergoing managerial development, both student and management alike should not lose sight of the primary aim of the program, which is the learning and potential development of the trainee, not departmental production. Even though there will be times that the trainee may be given specific responsibilities to oversee operations, clean guestrooms, or service public areas, advantage should not be taken of the trainee or the situation to the detriment of the development function. Development of new growth in the trainee becomes difficult when the training instructor or coordinator is not only developing a new manager but is also being held responsible for the production of some aspect of housekeeping operations.

Records and reports

Whether you are conducting a training or a development program, suitable records of training progress should be maintained both by the training supervisor and the student. Periodic evaluations of the student's progress should be conducted, and successful completion of the program should be recognized.

Public recognition of achievement will inspire the newly trained or developed employee to achieve standards of performance and to strive for advancement. Once an employee is trained or developed and his or her satisfactory performance has been recognized and recorded, the person should perform satisfactorily to standards. Future performance may be based on beginning performance after training. If an employee's performance begins to fall short of standards and expectations, there has to be a reason other than lack of skills. The reason for unsatisfactory performance must then be Sought out and addressed. This type of follow-up is not possible unless suitable records of training and development are maintained and used for comparison.

Evaluation and performance appraisal

Evaluation and performance appraisal for employees will occur as work progresses, it is not uncommon to find the design of systems for appraisal as part of organization and staffing functions. This is true because first appraisal and evaluation occurs during training, which is an activity of staffing. Once trainees begin to have their performance appraised, the methods used will continue throughout employment. As a part of training, new employees should be told how, when, and by whom their performances will be evaluated and should be advised that questions regarding their performance will be regularly answered.

Initial employment should be probationary in

nature, allowing the new employee to improve efficiency to where the designated number of rooms cleaned per day can be achieved in a probationary period (about three months). Should a large number of employees be unable to achieve the standard with that time, the standard should be investigated. Should only one or two employees be unable to meet the standard of rooms cleaned per day, an evaluation of the employee in training should either reveal the reason why or indicate the employee as unsuitable for further retention.

An employee who after suitable training cannot meet a reasonable performance standard should not be allowed to continue employment. Similarly, an employee who has met required performance standards in the specified probationary period should be continued into regular employment status and thus achieve a reasonable degree of security in employment.

Evaluation of personnel is an attempt to measure selected traits, characteristics, and productivity. Unfortunately, evaluations are generally objective in nature, and raters are seldom trained in the art of subjective evaluation. Initiative, self-control, and leadership ability do not lend themselves to measurement; therefore such characteristics are estimated. How well they are estimated depends to a great extent on the person doing the estimating. Two raters using the same form and rating the same person will probably arrive at different conclusions.

Certain policies on the use of evaluations should be established so that they are understood by both the person doing the evaluating and the person being evaluated. These policies must be established and disseminated by management. In order to establish such policies, the following questions, among others, must be answered and communicated to all those involved in the evaluation: What will evaluations be used for? Will evaluations influence promotions, become a part of the employee's record, be used as periodic checks, or be used for counselling and guidance? What qualities are going to be evaluated? Who is going to be evaluated? Who will do the evaluating? Reliable evaluations require careful planning and take considerable time, skill, and work. An evaluation must be understood by the employee.

Evaluation should be used at the end of a probationary period, and the employee must understand at the beginning of the period that he or she will be observed and evaluated. Each item, as well as what impact the evaluation will have on future employment, should be explained to the employee. People undergoing periodic evaluations, such as at the end of one year's employment, should also know why evaluations are being conducted and what may result from the evaluation. In both situations, the evaluation should be used for counselling and guidance so that performance may be improved upon or corrected if necessary. Certainly, strong points should be pointed out. An employee should be made aware of good as well as not-so-good evaluations.

Evaluations should be made for a purpose and not for the sake of an exercise. They should ultimately be used as management tools. Evaluations should be developed to fit the policies of the particular institution using it and the particular position being evaluated. The same evaluation may not be suitable for every position.

Operational planning

The subject of planning for the opening of a hotel has thus far included staffing, scheduling, preparing job descriptions, using materials, and hiring, orienting, and training employees. Even though the who, what, and when may have been decided, procedures for the bow of operations still remain to be established. The executive housekeeper may have, through past experience, established a mental plan of daily operations as they should be conducted. Much remains to be done, however, in standardizing specific procedures and routines for the new property.

Certain activities of direction and control must be planned for in advance of opening. These are delegating work (an activity of direction) and establishing reporting systems, developing performance standards, measuring results, and taking corrective action (activities of control). These activities cannot take place without having procedures designed and communicated to employees * Since most of the work of the housekeeping department is a routine that recurs on a daily basis, communication for direction and control is best done with forms. The day-to-day delegation of tasks as to which rooms require service and who will actually service them is performed through a routine commonly known as opening the house. This delegation takes place by the creation and use of several forms that are developed in advance of opening and are made available in sufficient quantity as to provide this communication on a daily basis.

Additional forms relating to communication, control of information about progress, and timely reporting of information are also necessary. Such forms usually are explained via documents known as standard operating procedures (SOPs). The SON not only establish and describe routines for normal daily operations, but they cover a variety of other procedures such as key control, room inspections, inventory procedures, standards of performance, and lost-and-found operations.

Procedures for opening the house

Opening the house is a procedure by which the following events take place.

1. Front desk provides information to housekeeping as to which rooms will require service on a given day.
2. Information received by housekeeping is transferred to working and control documents for senior GRAs (team leaders or supervisors) to use that day to control work progress.
3. Information is provided showing room sections with specific GRAs assigned and any open sections (sections with no GRAs assigned due to occupancy being less than 100 percent).
4. If occupancy is less than 100 percent, the information is used to establish 18-room worldoads for those GRAs who are scheduled to work on the specific day, This is accomplished by taking Occupied rooms from open sections and marking them as pickup rooms for GRAs whose regular sections are less than fully occupied. Total pickup rooms combined with the regular rooms of sections that are occupied form the 18-room workloads. (With 100 percent occupancy, all sections have GRAs assigned and there are no pickup rooms.)
5. After all occupied rooms have been assigned to a specific GRA and information is cross-checked on all team leader documents, the daily planning is transferred to documents, whereby GRAs are informed of individual work assigned.
6. Because the House Breakout Plan divided the model hotel into four divisions of five sections each, daily opening-the-house exercises require the preparation of 24 documents (forms) to convey information from the front desk to the workers and supervisors who will be responsible for performing the work.
7. Once all forms are properly filled out, placed on a clipboard, and positioned on the main linen room counter, room keys associated with appropriate work

areas are prepared for issue. When this is done, opening the house planning for that specific day is considered complete.

It is important to recognize that all planning relating to opening the house may be computerized, and the specific documents referred to in this section can be obtained through hotel computers.

Preparing for arrival of employees

Planning the workload distribution for the day has now been completed. Note that the forms used are in fact routine directives for the accomplishment of work for the day. They are the delegation of tasks to employees based upon the specific occupancy requirements for the servicing of guestrooms on a specific day. All that remains to be done now is to prepare for the arrival of employees.

A duplicate copy of the four senior GRA's work schedules are made and displayed on the linen room counter near the telephone and the electrowriter (an electrical device that transmits and receives facsimiles of handwritten messages between housekeeping, front office, and engineering).

Original Supervisors' Daily Work Reports are attached to clipboards and placed on the linen room counter to await employee arrivals at about 8:00 A.M. A copy of the GRA's, Daily Report for *open* sections is also attached to the senior housekeepers' clipboards. All other GRA's Daily Reports with pickups assigned are attached to smaller clipboards, along with a blank copy of the same form (to be used later in the day for a room report). Pass keys associated with work areas are put next to the clipboards on the linen room counter. Opening the house operations are now considered complete and the department awaits 8:00 A.M. and the arrival of employees for work.

Standardization

Standard operating procedures (SOPs) are written instruments that set forth specific recurring actions. They are the devices by which procedures are standardized and are the basis for ready reference as to how to accomplish specific tasks. The opening-the-house procedure just described is a prime example of a procedure requiring documentation.

The existence of an SOP on a given subject tacitly prevents deviation from standard activities until such time as a controlled change takes place. At that time a new or revised SOP may be promulgated. SON are similar in form, are numbered, and are usually kept in a reference journal (manual) available for anyone who will have any responsibility regarding a specific procedure. SOPs are coded into various departments of the hotel and may be collected into a master SOP notebook available to the general manager and others interested in reviewing operational techniques. All SOPs usually begin with a simple statement of policy, followed by paragraphs indicating directives, procedures, explanation of forms, records to be kept, positional responsibilities, and coordinating relationships.

Structured versus unstructured operations

Some managers feel that large numbers of controlled SOPs form an organization that is too highly structured, creating an environment that stifles initiative. On the contrary, organizations that do not have controlled processes and procedures usually have as many ways to perform an operation as there are people working at the tasks.

Some employees may present better ways of accomplishing a task than the manner prescribed in an SOP. If such is the case, testing of a new procedure may well warrant the promulgation of a change in procedure, again standardizing to the better way. SOPs can therefore present a challenge to employees to find better ways to accomplish tasks. If such participation results, employees may be given credit for their participation in improving operations.

Suitable subjects for standard operating procedures in hotels

The following procedural items are suitable for presentation by SOPs. Note that these procedures recur regularly, are suitable for delegation of tasks, allow for communication by forms, and are the foundation upon which change may be made if warranted.

— Opening the house
— Daily routine
— Night activities
— Key control
— Lost-and-found operations
— Inventory control procedures
— Linen-handling procedures
— Time card control
— Dilution control for chemicals used in cleaning
— Inspection checklists
— Standards of performance
— Maintenance work-order program
— Control Of guest loan items

The extent to which housekeeping department managers choose to document procedures for reference, standardization, and use in training is a matter of personal preference, and, in most cases, company Policy. Most companies requiring the promulgation of SOPs are usually quick to emphasize that such SOPs are to be used primarily as guidelines for operations and should not stifle initiative in the investigation of ways and means to improve operations. Many hotels are quick to reward employees who find better ways of performing tasks; some even offer incentive awards for improvement of procedures. The SOPs may very well become the framework for operations and, simultaneously, the tool whereby controlled change may take place.